SAVING FOR GOOD:
Adieu Maman

By
Genie Saffren

"Saving for Good: Adieu Maman," by Genie Saffren. ISBN 978-1-949756-67-8 (softcover); 978-1-949756-685 (eBook).

Published 2019 by Virtualbookworm.com Publishing Inc., P.O. Box 9949, College Station, TX , 77842, US.

©2019 Genie Saffren. All rights reserved. No part of this publication may be reproduced, stored in a retrieval system, or transmitted in any form or by any means, electronic, mechanical, recording or otherwise, without the prior written permission of Genie Saffren.

For Guy

Contents

Prologue v

Chapter 1: Bits and Pieces 1

Chapter 2: America 1922 - 1927 8

Chapter 3: David 1927 - 1946 10

Chapter 4: Les Morceaux d'une Vie 20

Chapter 5: Bordeaux, France 1883 – 1916 The Western Front 1916 – 1918 Biarritz, France 1918 - 1920 24

Chapter 6: Denise 1921 -1946 29

Chapter 7: D&D 33

Chapter 8: California 1946 - 1947 37

Chapter 9: Return to France, August – October 1950 40

Chapter 10: Pasadena 1950 – 1955 44

Chapter 11: The Move 1955 61

Chapter 12: Home Sick 1956 73

Chapter 13: Rotten Bananas 1957 81

Chapter 14: Buried Treasure 1958 92

Chapter 15: Check Mate 1959 102

Chapter 16: Teenager 1960 111

Chapter 17: Left Out 1961 126

Chapter 18: You Are Missing To Me 1962 131

Chapter 19: Happy Daze? 1963 156

Chapter 20: Love 1964 164

Chapter 21: Clutch 1965 172

Chapter 22: My Turn 1966 179

Epilogue 184

Prologue

I had a memory hiccup today. While cleaning out my now-grown children's closet, I found part of a collection of what I call *écusson* (emblem) patches that their Grandpa had accumulated on his many travels. It reminded me of when I was very young and used to look out the triangular-shaped window from the back seat of my dad's Oldsmobile. That little window had several colorful decals that he or Mom had moistened and slid onto the glass. They were souvenirs from the national parks, I think – Yosemite, Yellowstone.

Sometimes now, when I get up in the middle of the night, I realize that I have been dreaming, remembering. Images, thoughts linger in my semi-consciousness that I don't want to forget, something that I want to think more about when I am fully awake. I tell myself to write it down because I know by morning I'll likely forget what it was. I never do, though, and later I tell myself that I should have. When I'm not asleep, I often collect lines of words that resonate with me from articles, quotes, books – to inspire me, give me direction or maybe hold up a mirror so I might recognize myself. It seems that all my life I have been drawn to certain people who are willing to reflect back to me how I appear to them. I crave feedback from others. I was one of those strange children that couldn't wait for a report card, so that I might get another clue about who I was. The evaluation might have made me feel unhappy, but it was worth the risk. You see, my mother died when I was ten, and I don't remember her.

At times I think I must not have had a very happy childhood because I remember so little of it, and the memories I do have don't feel like my own but more like the dim recollection of a movie. Why are my memories so faded? I lived with my mother every day for over ten years. I should have a sense of her, what our relationship was like.

What made her laugh, what got her worked up – what was her favorite color? Am I anything like her?

My first memories? So many images in my head are probably of old photographs. My parents took a picture of me nearly every week of my life until my brother was born when I was almost six. I guess it didn't matter if they were my own memories or of those familiar snapshots, each one with captions my mom carefully wrote on the back, because either way, it wasn't enough.

When I was in college I worked for my father. One afternoon he walked up to my desk and placed an old velvet jewelry case and a leather handbag in front of me. Inside the case were several pieces of my mother's good jewelry. The handbag contained a wallet, glasses, a rosary, a small tin of Bayer aspirin: a tiny time capsule of the year 1957, the year my mother died. My father said nothing about the items, only that he had kept them in the factory vault. It was always like that. When the anniversary of her death would approach he'd sometimes ask me if I knew what day was coming, but he said little else. I longed for their story. But my father rarely talked to me about my mother, and broke off almost all contact with their friends and her family after she died.

In some ways it felt as if some part of my father had died too. He was like a ghost hiding from me at home pretending to be asleep under his Wall Street Journal. I sensed his sadness and difficulty managing me and my brother. Our family was broken and he wanted to fix it. Even as a ten year old I knew he was trying. Dad would give me wistful looks but he didn't talk about his feelings – it was as if he were still holding on to a dream and then he suddenly let it go. I always felt sorry for him and then felt guilty that I did, because he was my daddy and daddies always knew what to do. I craved attention, any kind of attention, just to prove to myself that I wasn't invisible, that I still existed and mattered and more importantly 'doing life' correctly.

After he remarried there was the complication of my stepmother. My real mother was never mentioned out loud again by anyone, including myself. It was as if she had vanished. My home became a new world that didn't include any reminders of her. No photographs of my mother were displayed. Anywhere. Her clothes, books, letters, everything disappeared. No trace was left of her. I couldn't put into words how angry and confused I was with my father. He shouldn't have let her disappear. But he was a hard man to rage against as a child, and later on as an adult. I tried to understand his inaction and finally figured that he just didn't know how to cope.

My father didn't keep her memory alive for me so I almost lost her.

When I still lived with my father and no one was home, I would scour the backs of drawers, look for boxes hidden in the garage, and even flip through pages of old books trying to find anything that belonged to my mother and my first ten years. Eventually, I did find old letters, three daily memoranda and an old valise filled with family photographs and films. But somehow I always came up with excuses not to really look at them. I had become the secret curator of these artifacts, unable to page through them, much less to study them and ask my father questions about them.

Most of the time I just lived my life. Occasionally I puzzled over how I might have grown up differently, if my mother had not died. Would I feel the same? Or would I have become more certain of who I was – or who I wanted to be? Then I would quickly shake off those thoughts and move on. Still, those feelings of being not quite connected to family, friends, and other people would always return. I was able to enjoy myself but I remained vigilant. I was really always hunting, longing for some new information about her. I still am.

I married at 22 to a gentle young man, a returning Vietnam soldier. Within three years of our wedding, we had two daughters. Becoming a mother stirred up all those feelings of loss and, more immediately, I felt unsure of myself as a mother. I was desperate for guidance, making it up as I went along. Was I doing it right? Thankfully, I was always able to recognize good role models when I came across them. I craved the company of a knowledgeable woman who could reassure me that what I was feeling and experiencing was normal. My greatest fear was that I would fail at being a mother.

When my father died, I was 45 years old. He was 80. Even after all that time, he never shared stories about her and I never asked. Maybe we both lacked the courage to bring it up. I felt that he still grieved and I protected him even when I really wanted him to open up. I had become just like him. Afraid.

All those questions never asked, answers never offered. All those lost opportunities for conversation. I realized this when he was alive, but I still couldn't ask. Maybe I didn't want to make him sad, reminding him of what we had all lost. I didn't get him to validate my few memories, fill in all those blank spaces. I kept hoping he would and part of me remained angry that he never did. I floundered.

Nine years later, my stepmother died. While emptying out their house, I found two large scrapbooks hidden deep in the garage. My dad had put together one book filled with small black and white photos that documented my mom and dad's first year together, and my mother filled the other with the love letters Dad wrote to her before they married. I never knew they existed. Discovering them made me feel so happy. I clutched each one like it was a talisman – even maybe - a key to my identity. I looked through the pages that day, touching but not reading them. I put the scrapbooks in a safe place, saving them for another time.

A dozen years after finding them, I finally sat down and read all the letters.

Maybe by piecing together all those keepsakes and souvenirs I will finally have a sense of who my mother was, as well as the essence of our relationship.

And perhaps that hollow space of things not known, not shared, not remembered, will diminish.

"Mommy" translated from French; author unknown

What miracle lives in a mother!
Others can love us
Only our mother understands us
She toils for us
Watching over us
Cherishes us
She forgives us for everything
She prays for us, and the
Only wrong she can ever do to us
Is to die
And abandon us...

Chapter 1:
Bits and Pieces

I sit cross-legged on the floor surrounded by bulging shoeboxes, an old valise and two large scrapbooks. Today I have time to sort through the detritus of several lives. Can I? Will I? I really need to – I've waited too long to learn about my family. They have been lurking close by for decades. No more excuses.

Young children don't question the make-up of their family. That's all they know. To them, however their family is, is. When I was about eight years old, I began to notice my friends' families – how they were the same, how they were different than mine. Many had living grandparents, lots of cousins. I only knew one of my grandparents and he died when I was nine. I had one cousin that lived close by. But there were two framed old photographs I remember seeing as a little girl: one was of my dad's mother, a stern looking bespectacled woman standing erect wearing an old fashioned outfit, and the other, a family picnicking in a field, squinting towards the camera. The family was my mother's: her parents, her and her sister with their two small dogs. Not much.

If I asked my dad about his youth he would often joke that he was born old and therefore couldn't remember a childhood. The little that he did say was that he was born in Poland and lived in a "hut" with dirt floors; that he once fell in a stream and couldn't swim and his mother died when he was only six years old. I knew that my mother's few relatives lived in France but she didn't talk about her background much, except that she was orphaned by age fifteen.

I open the shoeboxes and I am transported to another time and place. Most items are labeled in English, some in Polish or Yiddish. One box contains items that belonged to my dad's aunts and uncles. The other boxes are filled with my father's mementoes. I didn't realize how meticulous my dad was about saving the bits and pieces of his life. It seemed that he had saved every paper, souvenir, and photograph. I'd like to believe that my dad left those clues to help me answer the many questions we couldn't talk about when he was still alive. Perhaps if I learn some of my dad's story, I will be able to fill in the missing pieces of my mother's story too.

My Kanka, my grandfather, my father's father, couldn't speak much English so it wasn't very easy for him to share stories about my dad or the "old country". But we spent a lot of time together before I started school. I always felt special around him and much loved.

Within my dad's papers I find passports, photographs and postcards. I discover that Kanka and my dad were from a small village named Janów Sokolski and Kanka's real name was Chaim. I can begin to picture what their life might have been like.

My grandfather: Chaim Aronowski

The Village of Janów Sokolski, 1908 – 1927

Summer 1908. Chaim lives in a small village that straddles the boundary between Poland and Russia. And depending on the month he is either Polish or Russian, but he is also Jewish and second-class regardless. Although the village is small, the class system is strong. There aren't too many Jewish families; however even within those few families there are four classes of people: the rich, the educated and religious, the middle-class and the poor. Chaim is not religious. He is a member of a secular socialist group involved in the local Jewish community organization serving as quasi-mayor of the neighborhood.

At 24 he is a tanner by trade, tall, lean, and pleasant looking, and the second oldest of seven children. He, his parents, and brothers and sisters all live together in a large one-room cottage that has a hard-packed earthen floor, outdoor plumbing and only candles or kerosene for light. A central hearth divides the large room into a kitchen and a parlor. At night, the parlor becomes the main sleeping area. Two large doors, one in the front and one in the back, and a large attic complete the cottage's design. Behind the cottage, there is a coal bin, a compact vegetable garden, some chickens and their cow. Nearby a narrow stream trickles, in the spring it flows.

A large four-cornered water well is the centerpiece of Janów's town square. To the northeast, a rutted dirt lane leads to a large wooden synagogue topped by an octagonal dome. The Jewish cemetery is nearby. To the southeast the road leads to a church, a small inn and the railway station. Looking towards the setting sun you can see the pungent smoke from the chimneys of the tannery. An ancient forest embraces the village to the east.

During the week, Janów's town square is a busy place filled with farm stands of produce and animals. Vendors push handcarts along the stone paved street with all kinds of merchandise for sale. Once in a while, an organ grinder with a real parrot joins the lively crowd.

Octagon roof synagogue, Janów

Tzali is Chaim's older brother. Unlike Chaim, he is a very quiet, shy young man with a shock of white hair. He smiles but his eyes do not, traumatized by his service in the Russian army he stays home most of the time. However Chaim, his younger brothers Mozes and Feiwel, and his father Shmuel work together at the tannery every day except the Sabbath. They struggle most days to earn enough money to feed and clothe the large family. His mother, Chave (née Becker) cooks, cleans and cares for the three youngest children, the chickens and *Zeisele,* their milk cow, who often wanders into the kitchen. In addition, she manages the *myysan slwy*, the Mason jar, hidden in the pantry, where Chaim's father and brothers place their hard earned *wzor* and *złoty.*

In 1909 Chaim is formally introduced to Gisky Fajngoldow, a serious bespectacled young woman he has seen at one of his socialist meetings. She is "higher born" than he, educated as a pharmacist. Her father owns a whiskey distillery. She lives with her parents and four sisters and one brother. Chaim is intrigued by her interest in politics and knowledge of medicine. And Gisky is not shy: she asks about why he moves his left arm so carefully. Smiling, he explains that he slashed his upper arm in an accident at the tannery. She has a quick wit, but she doesn't flirt, and this Chaim finds pleasing.

Gisky Fajngoldow

Before long, Chaim realizes he has fallen in love. He asks Gisky to marry him. She loves Chaim but her family does not approve of the match. They consider him a poor man, beneath their daughter. Nevertheless they marry. Shunned by her own family, Gisky moves into the already crowded Aronowski home.

Living with Chaim's family proves no less treacherous. Gisky is regarded with suspicion. And in particular, Chaim's sisters do not trust her. But she keeps busy each day, working at the village apothecary shop until Chaim returns from the tannery. She is still an outsider to them, and soon their wariness turns to jealousy. Especially Pesra, Chaim's youngest sister, does not like Gisky or Chaim for marrying her. She tells a Russian officer that her brother has done something illegal. He is almost arrested because of his sister's false report.

Family tensions increase and make home life more uncomfortable for Gisky and Chaim. Chave's three daughters, Penina, Clara and Pesra, are all of marriageable age. However with no dowry, there are no suitors. The disappointed sisters become all the more jealous when Gisky becomes pregnant. On February 16, 1912 she gives birth to David. And two years later a daughter, Rachela, is born.

In spite of all the stresses, Chaim and Gisky are very happy with their little family. After each long day they reunite and climb up to the attic and listen to the house: "Zeyde", grandpa Shmuel, strumming on his mandolin in the parlor, the rise and fall of Chaim's sisters arguing and Mama sending them off to set the table, baby Rachela wailing on her hip. Sharing a smile, they follow the aromas back down. Taking Rachela from "*Bobeshi*" they join the whole family around the table for supper: lungen stew with a special treat of kielbasa and pickled herring.

Unfortunately, the world around their village becomes more and more hostile. The Russian Empire had started a process of liberalization a few years earlier but it did not last. Then Germany, in contrast, tried to force Poland to "Germanize". In Bialystok, less than 40 kilometers from Janów, 75 Jews were murdered by marauding Russian soldiers. Many Christian Poles helped hide Jewish families to protect them. However, the coming war will surround Poland and rip it apart, pitting Christian against Jew.

Penina, Chaim's oldest sister, wisely senses that Janów offers her a bleak future. Petite, attractive and quite independent, she writes to an uncle who lives in Germany asking to borrow money to buy a ticket to sail to America. At the same time, she also writes a distant cousin (*landsleit*, someone from Janów) who now lives along the Merrimack River in Haverhill, Massachusetts, working as an innkeeper. Penina asks if he is willing to sponsor her immigration and provide her work if she can make it to the United States.

Penina's parents are against this idea. They regard long-distance travel, especially from their tiny home to the unknown United States, dangerous and morally unfit for an unmarried young woman. They also fear that if she leaves Janów they will likely never see their daughter again. But Penina is headstrong and preserving. And after nearly a year of waiting, her uncle sends her the funds and she purchases her one-way ticket. In early 1914, at 17 years of age, she says goodbye to her family.

Penina travels to America by horse and wagon, on several trains, and finally by steam ship in a smelly, cramped and claustrophobic steerage compartment. But once she sets foot in her new world she knows she has made the right decision. She travels on to Haverhill and immediately begins working in her cousin's boarding house. It is here that she meets the man she will eventually marry. His name is Max Grossman and he is a shoemaker.

Penina will never return to Janów. But because of her bold move, she will be able to sponsor her brother Feiwel and eventually the rest of her siblings as they make their way from Poland to America. She will change the course of her family's history.

One spring morning in 1915, Janów awakens to the sound of tolling church bells. They ring for a long time. Shmeul comes home to say it is an alarm for war: the Germans are driving the Russians out of 'Russian Poland'. Soon the sounds of bombardment, maybe 25 kilometers away can be heard. Petty family problems recede and everyone wonders if and when the war will arrive in their village. Predictably Pesra grows more frantic, complaining of frailty, wailing that everyone is against her.

Although Janów is not directly in a war zone, the villagers, especially the Jewish population, feel a heightened sense of unease. Some months they feel more autonomous but as the provisional governments struggle back and forth, their gains are abruptly withdrawn. Promises are made and then broken.

In August of 1918, Gisky is suddenly taken ill along with others in the Aronowski cottage. Three days later, she dies of the "Bolshevik *kholere*" (the Bolshevik disease), the Spanish Influenza. Everyone else in the family survives. Gisky is only 28 years old. Little David stands with his father, listening to the prayers for his dead mother. He doesn't understand. He is six and half years old. His grandmother will now care for him and his little sister. Chaim is devastated.

Life becomes increasingly unhappy and stressful, both inside the cottage and in their village. The frequent movement of armies over the last four years, and the widespread uncertainty concerning Jewish sympathies have created even more tension, as some Jews are suspected of being Bolshevik agents. Coupled with the scarcity of food and fuel, life is uneasy at best.

Within five years Chaim's father dies and all of Chaim's brothers and sisters leave Janów for a new life in America. Only Chaim, his mother, and his children remain in Poland.

Simple day-to-day existence becomes very uncomfortable for anyone who is Jewish. Neighbors, as well as Russian revolutionary types are unpredictable. The family does not feel safe. David is almost 15 and at risk of being conscripted into the Russian army. Finally, Chaim realizes he and his family, must leave Janów. His mother feels she is too old to make the voyage. He embraces her goodbye. She will never see her children or grandchildren again.

If relocation proves necessary and wise, it all comes at a great price. The seven siblings will lose all connection with any relatives left behind in Europe.

Chapter 2:
America 1922 - 1927

It is 1922. Three years earlier, Penina - who renamed herself Pearl - husband Max and their four year old daughter Marcella, move from Massachusetts to Rochester, New York. Feiwel, 21, Chaim's youngest brother, sails to America. He joins his sister and her family at 88 Aurora Street. Max is the foreman at the Rochester Shoe Fitting Company and is able to get Feiwel a job working as a shoe-fitter assembling baby shoes and gloves. Two by two, Mozes, Tzali, then Pesra and Clara follow, all reunite in Rochester and, through Max, find employment at the same factory.

RMS Ausonia, Montreal, Canada

After the sad and stressful process of gathering all the necessary papers, signatures and photographs, Chaim finally purchases three one-way third-class tickets. Unlike his siblings, Chaim must choose a Canadian shipping company because the United States has cut immigration from Central Europe, making Canada more accessible. Besides, the opportunity to separate himself from his brothers and sisters seems itself appealing. His little family travels by several trains to reach Cherbourg, France, where they board the RMS Ausonia to Southampton England, then they steam across the Atlantic to Montreal, Canada. It is early 1927.

Unfortunately, it is soon apparent that Montreal is an overcrowded city for poor "green" Jewish immigrants from Poland. Their tiny flat has cold running water, but no toilet or bath. Tuberculosis is rampant. Jobs are scarce. And the local government makes it imperative to place David and Rachela in a French-speaking school, not even a Hebrew school. In fact, they are enrolled in a Catholic school. Feeling less than welcome, they almost immediately begin to make plans to join their family in the United States.

Eight months later they are allowed to enter and travel to Malone County, New York. They settle in Rochester at 54 Buchan Park near Chaim's brothers and sisters.

At first, Rochester is overwhelming. The noise alone: the sounds of cars, trolleys honking and clanging, people talking and shouting. So many strange names swirling around: Lindbergh, Coolidge, Dempsey, Babe Ruth. What does it all mean? As in Montreal, the pace and the sheer number of people are shocking. But it feels different, somehow. If not more welcoming, then certainly more comfortable. But what is also more and more apparent is how rich this new land is. It is as if they travelled forward in time. Chaim realizes how very grateful he feels to have family already in place to help him, David and Rachela figure everything out.

Soon he joins his brothers at the Rochester Shoe Fitting Company.

Chapter 3:
David 1927 - 1946

David, 15 years old, is enrolled in public school. He quickly learns to speak, read and write English, and he thrives. A school administrator describes him as a sensitive boy with 'an imaginary rather than materialistic outlook.' When he enters Rochester East High School, he writes short plays, paints sets for various theatre productions, takes up photography, and is attracted to the young socialist movement. At one of its club meetings he meets Jimmy Fantauzzo. Jimmy is two years older than David and takes him under his wing. They will become life-long friends.

Together, David and Jimmy become political activists, with strong left leanings and nearly utopian goals. They help organize basket weavers to create a union, write letters to local and state officials, and get involved in demonstrations. They both manage to get on the list of the "most prominent and most active members in the Communist Party and Sympathizers" in the Rochester area.

When they are not "organizing," David and Jimmy stroll down busy Joseph Avenue, visit Keilson's Drugstore for an ice cream, or jump on the trolley and ride all the way down to Charlotte Beach. Or they just watch the pretty girls walk by. Even their politics entail a youthful slapstick element. During one of their adventures, they somehow lock themselves in the Rochester Communist Party headquarters after hours and have to be rescued by the fire department! Little wonder how their names landed on Rochester's official list of Communist Party members and sympathizers.

In spite of his many extra-curricular activities, David proves to be a very good student. He graduates and is accepted to the University of Rochester, even though there is an eight percent "Jewish quota;" his major is in mechanical engineering. He dons his freshman "beanie" and happily becomes part of university life. At first he does well. But by the middle of his second year, he is near the bottom of his class and is put on probation. Finally, in early 1932, he withdraws. Why David fails to realize his obvious academic promise may be linked to the country's worsening economic condition that focuses more and more of his attention on his socialist activities.

Despite the serious economic downturn, Uncle Feiwel is able to open his own shoe factory, The Gar Shoe Corporation. With his profits, he and his brothers and sisters can choose to relocate. And with none having yet married, they once again live together, this time in Chicago.

It is November 1933.

Feiwel, standing far left; Gar Shoe Corporation factory floor

Chaim decides to remain in Rochester. Again, he desires to be independent of his brothers and sisters. And he wants to provide David a chance to return to school. To make all this possible, he finds work at another shoe factory.

By late 1934 the factory has shuttered. Chaim, using his small savings, decides to try something completely different. He opens a tiny grocery store and the family and their orange cat Houdini move into the second floor apartment that sits above 492 Monroe Avenue. In the back of the shop, David sets up a small lending library, with many socialist titles. He charges a penny a loan. In addition to working at the grocery, David goes door-to-door trying to sell McCall's magazine subscriptions.

Chaim, interior grocery store

But the depression continues to deepen. Even together, the store's income and David's part-time job cannot support the family. Rachela works in the store but contributes little. Sadly, David cannot afford to return to the university. The nearly $500 fee for annual tuition and books is far beyond his means.

By the late '30s, Feiwel's shoe business is thriving and he opens a factory in Los Angeles, California. He and his siblings move from Chicago to southern California, as well as Pearl and her youngest daughter, Evelyn. Sadly, Pearl's husband Max has died from the lingering effects of injuries sustained in a serious car accident. Feiwel will help support them and he rents them an apartment on Alta Vista Avenue. Clara decides to live by herself nearby.

Feiwel, his brothers and Pesra live at the El Royale apartments on stylish Rossmore Avenue.

Marcella, Pearl's oldest daughter, now married, remains back East near Chaim, David and Rachela.

Feiwel, who has legally changed his name to Philip Aronov, can provide David, Rachela and Chaim good paying jobs *if* they move across the country to Los Angeles.

Even though it's a continuous struggle, David and his family decide to stay put. He busies himself with his political activism but still yearns to return to the university. Unhappily, he recognizes that he is now probably too old to be a student.

In January 1937 David becomes a naturalized citizen of the United States and legally changes his name to David Aronoff. But if anything, his official citizenship status only heightens his awareness of anti-immigrant and anti-Jewish feelings in Rochester. He reads a disturbing anti-Semitic pamphlet circulating around the city, and listens to the radio broadcasts of a Catholic priest, Father Coughlin, whose sermons encourage religious hatred. By late 1939, Coughlin has become a very popular advocate of Nazi policies and violence against Jews.

In the face of this fierce and populist anti-Semitism, David proves fearless. He writes many letters to Jewish leaders and city officials demanding that the radio station stop broadcasting Coughlin. He helps coordinate an interfaith group that works to combat anti-Semitism and creates and distributes informational handbills.

In May of 1941, on behalf of his Communist organization, he writes directly to President Roosevelt, imploring him to free an American political prisoner and keep the US out of the war in Europe and work toward peace instead.

By the summer, with the economy still shaky, Chaim is forced to close the grocery store. Reluctantly, he and Rachela leave Rochester for a fresh start in Los Angeles. Meanwhile, David manages with his cousin Marcella and her husband's help to purchase an old jalopy to drive across the country. Traveling alone helps him realize that he can picture a life for himself separate from his family. He dreams of opening a small photography studio.

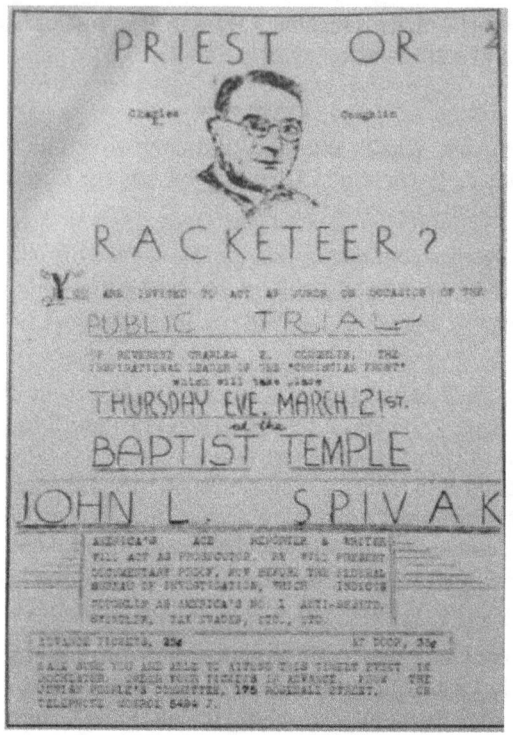

When Chaim and Rachela first arrive in Los Angeles and look for a place to rent, they are disturbed and discouraged to see signs in apartment windows that warn "no dogs, no peddlers, no jews" (sic). However, their very rich Uncle Philip is able to find them an apartment on Hayworth Avenue. Almost immediately they begin working at Philip's new shoe factory on Raymond Street in Pasadena. And again, they find themselves adjusting to another new place, with new people.

David arrives a month later. He tries very hard to find any job dealing with photography or art. After several weeks of dead ends, he grudgingly gives up and accepts a job working for his uncle. Far more perversely, he is hired as a union buster. It is beyond ironic. But he adapts: he joins the local chapter of the Communist party and becomes its secretary. And he has enough extra money to buy his own camera, a 35-millimeter Balda.

He soon discovers there is an active labor movement in Los Angeles. As he wanders through the quaint tourist attraction of Olvera Street downtown, he watches cobblers turning out handmade woven leather sandals, hammering and pounding without the modern machines his uncle has at the shoe factory. Nearby in Pershing Square, David finds himself 'at home' participating in lively debates full of impassioned speakers. Even if he can't work in a Union shop, he can organize others so that they can have better working conditions, shorter hours and higher wages.

He also learns what many others have already realized: Los Angeles is a paradise. The weather is almost perfect. The setting is unbelievable with beaches, mountains and deserts and hundreds of miles of highway to explore it all. Before long, he joins a group of New York State natives who arrange huge home state picnics. David attends his first in October. There, he meets people who like himself, are trying to create new lives for themselves in Los Angeles. It truly is the land of opportunity.

As David struggles to take advantage of his new city's blessings, he despairs that he is still living with and working for his family. It pains him to see others weave beautiful lives around their families, only to find a narrow and dissatisfied family for himself. He wonders how his family can still be so unhappy, bitter and jealous.

Two years pass. It's April 1943 and David is inducted into the US Army. The country has been at war for nearly eighteen months, and he is 31 years old. He does not believe in the war but admits that this is the one sure way he can separate from his family.

David (second from right)

After basic training, David's unit is sent to Northern Ireland in February 1944. They then move to an Allied camp outside of Warminster, England on the Salisbury Plain.

He stands outside his tent, scanning the empty land, probably cut from farmers' fields. The only landmark, a low hill topped with a small band of trees. The air is clear, crisp with cold.

Warminster, England

On September 14, the 47th Reinforcement Battalion leaves England and boards troop ships bound for the coast of France, to Le Havre. There, David and his fellow soldiers are loaded onto every conceivable type of transportation for the slow move northward: two and a half ton open trucks, dump trucks, and huge pontoon trucks. They are issued K-rations for the trip and warned there would be no stop so if they had to relieve themselves the best way would be from the moving trucks. The convoy drives for hours. The men are confused, anxious, cold and wet.

Finally they bivouac (are provided temporary quarters) in the small village of Noyon, located in northern France near the frontier. It is freezing cold, but the soldiers are promised movies, night passes and hot meals. But confusion reigns: duffle bags are lost, no one has been issued cold-weather footgear and soldiers must exchange their pistols for M-1 rifles that most do not know how to load.

The US Army takes over a small hotel as their command post. The troops are housed in cottages, barns or hastily built structures. David's squad stays in an old stable. He removes one glove so he can touch the smooth, worn wood that frames the doorway. The grain of the unpainted surface caresses his fingers. The ground is covered in snow and mud.

The troop's destination is the Ardennes forest in Belgium where they are to join several other American and English companies in their counterattack on the German army. They are the army infantry replacements.

Noyon, France

It is here, while waiting for orders that fate may have played a pivotal role. While sitting on a toilet in the latrine, David pulls the flush chain. The chain tears the tank off the wall and the tank falls on the back of his head, knocking him unconscious. When his company pulls out, he must stay behind in a field hospital with a concussion and infection. His company goes to the front, Elsenborn Ridge, the Battle of the Bulge. Many of his comrades are killed.

He slowly recovers, rejoins his company and travels south to Paris. They arrive on April 11. Victory over Germany seems imminent, and on May 8 after almost six years of deprivation and unimaginable loss, the World War II Allies formally accept the unconditional surrender of Nazi Germany, ending the war in Europe. David and his buddies join the crowds streaming through the streets, moving towards the Champs Elysees and the Arc de Triomphe. There, he takes a photo as the huge Nazi flag is ripped from under the arch.

On July 2 David is sent to the southwest of France on the Atlantic coast, to Biarritz. The US Army has taken over several hotels, casinos, and villas along the Grand Plage and converts them into a vocational education campus, The American Army University. Presumably leaders make these changes to keep the troops occupied and out of trouble since they are no longer needed on the battlefield. As a staff sergeant, David, is assigned to train soldiers in office skills.

It is here that he meets the young woman who will become my mother.

La Grande Plage, Biarritz July 1945

Chapter 4:
Les Morceaux d'une Vie

I drag the old valise closer to where I sit. It's covered in what looks like crocodile skin, with two brass latches. Several ship labels decorate the sides. I open it and immediately I am struck by the odor, not exactly musty but memorable somehow. Inside I find four small leather photo albums, three red daily memoranda's and several loose papers. They all belonged to my mother. I recognize her small, neat handwriting. She captioned every black and white photo, many with lengthy explanations of color, texture, or design of the subjects – most with frank appraisals of the people pictured. Some are written in English but most in French. I open the journals and realize each one represents one year: 1955, 1956 and 1957. Underneath it all, I find several sepia toned photos mounted on board with fancy embossed words. Thankfully most have dates. I literally start laying out everything by date, slowly assembling the pieces of my mother's story.

Biarritz, France 1882 – 1908

Maria Simon, 16, is the eldest of seven children. Her mother, Jeanne, gives birth to her youngest brother and dies in the process. Maria takes on the bittersweet task of caring for the infant, who is named Louis. When her little brother is about six months old, she returns to work at the family dressmaking *atelier* on the fashionable Rue de Mazagran in Biarritz, France. Baby Louis comes along, too. He grows up surrounded by seamstresses.

Biarritz appears at first glance to be made of one wide street with hotels, cafes and casinos to the left and right. Well-heeled ladies and gentlemen walk about the hotel gardens that slope downwards to the high cliffs that overlook the broad expanse of the Bay of Biscay on the

Atlantic coast of the French Basque country. Many people come for the "waters," the salt water cures for ailments as varied as tuberculosis, rheumatism and mental imbalance.

All who visit or live here, though, are mesmerized by the sound, the perfume, the rhythm of the sea.

Ocean waves beat on jagged rocks and cliffs, roaring and surging past the sweep of the coarse yellow sand beach. From the time of Napoleon, Biarritz is regarded as *la reine des plages et la plage des rois* - the queen of beaches and the beach of kings. It is a paradise.

Ten years pass. It is February 1892. A few days before her 26th birthday, Maria marries Bernard Hitze, a Basque cabinetmaker, an *ébénist*. He repairs and purchases everything crafted in wood for the posh Hôtel du Palais, whose wide doors open to the beach.

Hôtel de Palais

Within five years they have two daughters, born two years apart, Gracieuse, and Jeanne. The family becomes quite prosperous. They live in a large compound at the crossroads of the rue de Vaureal and rue Michelet. It is three stories of white washed stone capped with red tiles, sitting on an entire city block with a large central courtyard, all within sight of the sea.

Even though Maria is busy raising her two children and her "baby" brother, she is still able to oversee the now very chic Simon couturier shop. No longer are the only workers her immediate family, there are a dozen seamstresses and tailors busily working at tables: sewing on machines, stitching by hand, ironing or draping fabrics on mannequins. Dressmaking becomes second nature to Maria. She designs all the shop's apparel, crafting her own patterns. And she is a good boss. Maria is an independent, modern woman with a playful sense of humor and a devilish opinion on most subjects.

Stepping outside, Maria stands in front of her shop, watching a bee fly through the large blue Hortensia blossoms. The sun is a shock of gold, glinting through trees that reach across the street, bent by the Mistral winds. Bernard walks up from the hotel to join her for the mid-day meal. He smells faintly of beeswax and linseed oil. They join hands and cross the street for home.

In early 1908, Maria organizes the wedding festivities for "baby" Louis, including the creation of both the bride and groom's costumes. As she peeks behind the door making sure everything is perfect, the photographer squeezes the shutter.

Chapter 5:
Bordeaux, France 1883 – 1916
The Western Front 1916 – 1918
Biarritz, France 1918 - 1920

Maria Caliot and Pierre Noguès marry in Bordeaux in 1883. Pierre is a railroad engineer. Within two years their first child is born, a son. Maria wants to baptize him Marcel, but Pierre does not approve. Without Maria's knowledge, Pierre registers the baby's name "Jean Leopold" at the city hall and at their parish church. Maria refuses to call him by that name and from that day on he *is* Marcel. Two years later their second son is born. They have no argument about his name. He is called Henri.

Marcel is a good student but his passion is for the church. His mother's brother is an abbot who encourages him and guides him. After his first communion, Marcel carefully inscribes in his small leather bound volume of "*L'Imitation de Jesus-Christ*" his wish to always be a good Christian.

It is 1916. France has been at war with Germany for nearly two years. Although Marcel had already served seven years earlier, he is again conscripted into the French army. He is 30 years old, tall, dark and rather serious looking. He was a *diacre,* a deacon, preparing to become a priest but now finds himself a stretcher-bearer in the middle of a scarred battlefield on the Western Front. He will spend almost the next two years of his life slogging, knee deep, through trenches, enduring days of paralyzing fear.

In late summer 1917, while struggling to lift a wounded soldier Marcel hears a swish and a strange wobbly sound passing over his head. It sounds different than the normal artillery noises. He smells what he thinks is garlic, but soon his eyes and throat burn. He cannot breathe. He and hundreds of other French troops gasp and writhe in pain. The Germans have lobbed canisters of a toxic chemical. Marcel and other victims are slowly transported to an army tent hospital. It is located in the small village of Noyon.

Marcel is devout, wanting to do God's work but by the war's end he returns home to Bordeaux a greatly changed man, shaken by his horrifying experiences and physically damaged by his exposure to mustard gas. Marcel will not return to the seminary and instead follows in his father's line of work and becomes a railroad engineer. Driving the steam trains back and forth from Bordeaux to Biarritz help him escape his haunting memories; he loses himself within the great puffs of steam, the screech of the wheels, and deep roar of the engines. Each day as he pulls into the Biarritz railway station he stares up at the large image of a dark lady with earrings and a heavy smile painted on the wall beneath the words "La Négresse".

Front, Gare de la Négresse (railway station), Biarritz

One Saturday Marcel decides to remain in Biarritz for the weekend. It is May 1919 and the casinos have finally re-opened after the Armistice. The owners are trying to attract wealthy visitors back to Biarritz and have financed a small airline company to operate as an air taxi between Bordeaux and Biarritz. Today they are offering "joy rides" over the Bay of Biscay and crowds have gathered to watch. Marcel notices the spooked horses and watches the dozens of pigeons released from the aero-plane, but his attention is fixed on a beautiful young woman.

The next day he attends mass and recognizes the same woman sitting a few rows in front of him. As soon as he receives communion, Marcel hurries outside, spots her and formally introduces himself. She is called Gracieuse Hitze. She has delicate features, lovely hands, wavy chestnut brown hair and green eyes. She lives nearby with her family at La Maison Hitze/ Chalet Jeanne and works as a seamstress at the family dressmaking shop on the Rue Mazagran.

Marcel is captivated by Gracieuse. He is 33 years old and has found love, something he was not expecting. She is much younger than he, but she is quickly enthralled with him and his deep, husky voice. Marcel is introduced to her parents and soon after they begin their courtship.

Not quite a year later, on April 22, 1920, they wed in a large ceremony at the church where they first met, St. Eugenie, surrounded by their extended family and friends. After the concluding rite, the new couple emerges through the wide doors that face the ocean.

Saving for Good | **27**

They turn, follow a path strewn with flowers and pine boughs into the courtyard of the Maison Hitze, their future home, for a family portrait and celebration.

Marcel and Gracieuse

Chapter 6: Denise 1921-1946

Marcel and Gracieuse's first child, Denise (*Nisou*), is born on May 8, 1921. Three years later her sister Marie Claire (*Mayie*) is born. The family is content, living by the sea in a resort town that is frequented by wealthy visitors from Europe and America.

Denise, Maman, Mayie, Tante Jeanne

But within fifteen years that happiness crumbles, and Denise and Mayie's comfortable lives are turned upside down. Death has shadowed the close-knit family. One by one, everyone dear to the girls dies. First their mother's sister, *Tante* Jeanne; next Grandmama Maria Hitze; two years later, their father succumbs to the insidious effects of the gas poisoning. Finally, and heartbreakingly, their mother begins to feel unwell. Within a few months she dies painfully of ovarian cancer. Denise and Mayie are left in the care of their father's brother, *Tonton* Henri Noguès and his wife *Tante* Germaine, who have no children of their own.

Soon it is clear that their aunt and uncle cannot or perhaps will not manage the girls' care, and they send them to a nearby children's home run by the Catholic Church. Once there, Mayie sobs uncontrollably and will not eat. Reluctantly, Henri Noguès and Germaine take her back, but they leave Denise behind at the home. She is fifteen, and remains there for almost three years, completing her secondary education. Almost daily, she writes to her sister and her cousin, Jean-Louis Simon. She reads poetry and becomes more and more immersed in her Catholic faith. But she feels utterly abandoned.

Denise, age 15

It is September 1939, and another war in Europe has begun. Denise, 18 years old, moves into the nearby *Pouponniere de L'Ermitage* to begin training as a childcare worker; she completes the program within one year, receiving high marks.

La Pouponniere de L'ermitage (interior), Villa "Castellmare", Biarritz

She continues to care for young children, working as an au pair for a wealthy family.

By late June 1940, France agrees to an armistice with Germany. Soon Biarritz becomes part of the occupied *zone nord* under the control of the Nazis. Denise, like everyone else, learns to make do with less food and fuel and to deal with new regulations that ban singing the Marseillaise, flying the French flag or watching American movies. No one can be out on the streets after 10 p.m. and everyone must set their clocks forward one hour to German time. Ugly concrete gun emplacements are built on the sand around Biarritz to protect the beaches from the Allies.

The German *Wehrmacht* takes over all the hotels and casinos, including the Hôtel du Palais. In *la Rotonde*, the grand dining room facing the ocean where Denise's grandfather once lovingly maintained the furniture, now displays a grotesque exhibit entitled "The Jews and France." One poster proclaims the many "methods" Jews have used to pervert French culture and spirit. Several of the French locals seem sympathetic to this view.

In January 1943 Denise decides to relocate to Paris so she can continue her education. She attends nursing school, where she lives during the week. On Friday afternoons she packs her small valise and stays with her cousin Jean-Louis (Lou Lou) and his wife Louisette in their apartment. On Monday morning she returns to school. Denise is 21 years old.

The German army has occupied the city for nearly three years. They have closed much of the Metro, periodically cut off electricity, and severely rationed food and goods. All French men must register for forced labor, but as a result of an old rugby injury Lou Lou cannot bend his left knee and receives a special dispensation.

In spite of the war and the subsequent shortages, Denise is happy. She loves being near her cousins, who are just as pleased to have her with them. Denise has found a sanctuary.

She continues with her studies and also gets a part-time job in a boarding school as a nurse's aide working with very young children, many who have been injured or are crippled. She contributes her earnings to her cousins, although there is little food or fuel to be found. But Denise is plucky and often goes out after the 8 p.m. Paris curfew to buy black market goods. On one foray she gets a tip that there's a ham available. Unfortunately, after money is exchanged Denise is given a live piglet! She dashes back to the apartment with her "ham" under her dark blue wool nurse's cape. Now there is another mouth to feed. They continue to eat asparagus, the only fresh food available for weeks.

Paris is liberated at last in August 1944. Denise, her cousins and her friends join the throngs that celebrate in the streets. But there are still German snipers hiding in some of the buildings. Shots ring out, echoing over the crowd. A bullet passes through Denise's cloak, barely missing her body.

Chapter 7:
D&D

I have possessed the two large black scrapbooks for a long, long time. I was so happy, excited to first find them and then to realize that my parents were the kind of people that would create a memorial of their love affair. That surprised me. That it took me nearly 15 years to finally read them also surprised me. But then again, I guess I had become a lot like my dad: afraid of how I would feel if I scratched too deep. Maybe it would hurt too much.

Leafing through the pages of my mother's scrapbook, I find dozens of love letters my father wrote to her during their courtship. Each one was carefully mounted onto the black pages. Folded between the back cover of the scrapbooks are three sheets of monogramed stationery detailing their journey across the Atlantic to the United States. I'd like to think that my mother was putting all her words, her feelings down on paper because she thought someone, like me, would cherish reading them years later.

In late June 1945 Denise is able to take a holiday and go back home to Biarritz. She stays with her uncle and aunt who now live at the Maison Hitze, which has been converted into several small apartments. A few days later Denise joins some old friends to relax on the beach and reminisce. She is sunning herself on the sand in front of the Casino Bellevue. David Aronoff, wearing his US Army uniform, steps out from the casino's large glass-paned doors for his lunch break. He strolls down to the sand and looks out onto the waves, and when he hears laughter he turns and stares at Denise. She grins directly at him. She speaks no English, and David speaks little French. It is summer. He is smitten. She seems interested in him. He thinks she has great legs and a beautiful smile.

During the next four weeks the two spend many hours together. But Denise must return to Paris for her final nursing exams. They promise to write to each other. With the help of a fellow GI, David writes in French to "Nisou" and their relationship grows.

It's Sept. 2, 1945 and World War II is over at long last. David is eager to be discharged from the Army. Although he is anxious to return to the United States, he has also fallen in love. He continues to write Denise from Biarritz, often twice a day, encouraging her to learn to speak English. When she writes of their possible future together, she worries about their different backgrounds. But David is so eager for her love that at first he's less than honest. When he tells her about himself, he writes that he is a Protestant. He's afraid if she learns that he's Jewish she will no longer be interested in him. "This is a new world, with new ideas," he writes Denise.

Finally David receives permission for a few days furlough, and takes a train to Paris. He can hardly wait to be with Denise again. They spend four wonderful days together. Denise introduces David to her cousins, and they visit Versailles and have a K-ration picnic. There the young lovers carve their initials on a wall outside the palace.

All too soon David must return to Biarritz but he immediately requests another leave for the end of the year.

By mid-October Denise learns that she passed her nursing examinations and accepts a job at the Claude-Bernard Hospital in Paris. She moves out of her cousins' apartment and into the hospital's dormitory, and begins working. She also starts taking formal English lessons. David is delighted when she writes of this wonderful news.

In early December, David says in a letter that, "I like Christmas, but I'm not religious at all." A few days later he implores Denise not to follow him blindly to the United States. Finally on Dec. 23, he writes of his strong love for her but admits there are some important things about himself that he has neglected to share: he is a naturalized American citizen, his parents are Jewish, but he does not believe in religion, and he is a Communist. David will understand if she cannot accept these things, but he will always love her. He also explains he does not believe in the French approach to marriage, which expects the wife to be subservient to her husband. Rather, he believes marriage is a partnership. A few days later Denise writes that her uncle Noguès probably would not approve of their marriage but that she loves David nonetheless.

David receives a two-week leave. Unfortunately, Denise cannot take time off from her new job so he is only able to spend a few hours with her. He travels on to Switzerland. But on his return trip to Biarritz he stops in Paris to see her again. They celebrate New Year's Eve together.

In January David responds to her worry about the faith of any children they might have together, "They (the children) should choose for themselves". He reassures her that his family in America will love her as he does, even though he has yet to write them about Denise. She tells him how depressed she feels when she is separated from him. David wonders if her uncle is pressuring her.

Lou Lou, while very happy for Denise, is concerned David may already be married, with a wife back in America. He suggests to Denise that they should be married in Paris. When Denise shares Lou Lou's worry, David quickly and happily agrees.

David learns the US Army requires a soldier who intends to marry a foreign wife find a civilian job and work for six months before a "war bride" can immigrate to the States. David hopes the rules will change. And they do. At last on March 30, David is discharged from the army and leaves Biarritz for Paris and his beloved Denise.

Less than a month later, on a beautiful spring morning, David and Denise are married by a Catholic priest on the steps of a church in the 4th *arrondisment* in Paris, witnessed by Lou Lou, Louisette and an army buddy of David's. They exchange simple gold rings engraved with "D.A. – D.N. 20 - 4 - 1946" inside. David promises to let their children be baptized Catholic. In spite of his beliefs, Denise is able to receive the sacrament of marriage. It is Saturday, the day before Easter.

David is somehow able to find and hire an ancient taxi that takes the newlyweds to the Parc des Buttes Chaumont for photographs and a picnic of ham and asparagus.

That night they stay at Hôtel Paris-Rome, in the 9th on the Rue de Provence. They honeymoon in the south of France, touring Pau, Biarritz and St. Jean de Luz. "Nisou" is effervescent, and so content. She happily introduces her new American husband to her friends and relatives and guides him all over her childhood haunts. Regrettably, she can only introduce David to her sister via letters. Mayie is living in Algeria. Denise will not be able to embrace her sister goodbye.

One glorious month later, David books two tickets on the SS Uruguay, the last ship commissioned by the US Army to take GI's home from France. Standing on the upper smoking deck, they watch the sad ruins of the harbor fade away. Denise is ecstatic. It is June 1946. She is 25 and he is 34.

Chapter 8:
California 1946 - 1947

After arriving in New York on June 29 the newlyweds travel across country by train to Los Angeles. Denise is enthralled with all the sights. The vastness of the country, the variety in the landscapes, even the smells – everything is larger, more magnificent than anything she had imagined. David, now called Dave by Denise or as she pronounces it *"Dove,"* is happy and so in love.

A few days after they arrive in Los Angeles, Dave takes his new bride to meet some of his family members. Uncles Philip, Morris (Mozes) and Charlie (Tzali) and his Aunts Pauline (Pesra) and Clara now live all together on a large estate in Arcadia, on Singing Wood Drive near the Santa Anita Racetrack. Driving down the long tree-lined entry is a bit intimidating but very impressive to Denise. The car stops, and Dave opens her door. There, like a row of Russian nesting dolls, await his aunts and uncles on the veranda. Denise, wearing one of only two dresses she travelled with and her sturdy nurse's shoes, literally bows down to shake each of their hands. She towers over them at 5 feet 7 inches tall. Charlie, the tallest, is 5 foot 4. Philip is barely 5 feet. He lets them rent an apartment he owns in Beverly Hills on Shirley Place and gives them a plot of land in Pasadena atop a hill as a wedding present. He is an eccentric but generous little man.

When Dave introduces Denise to his father, it is love at first sight. Chaim, now called Haskel, can't speak much English, let alone French, but somehow they manage. Denise's laughter and cooking capture his heart. He is happy – for his son, for himself. He gives them a black and white cat, which they name Mitou, as a wedding gift.

The next day "Nisou" tells "Dove" that she needs underwear, specifically panties. They must go shopping. Gamely Dave takes her to a department store and they enter the lingerie section where he explains to the saleswoman what Denise is telling him in French. Things he would never do before he knew Denise, he does now. He is not afraid of what other people may think. She makes him brave.

Taking advantage of the G.I. Bill, Dave gets a loan to build a home on the property Philip has given them. There is only one gravel road leading up to what will become Sequoia Drive. It takes nearly nine months to build the house, just about the same time it takes Denise to produce their first child: I am born on May 31, 1947.

Sequoia Drive, Pasadena

Chapter 9:
Return to France, August – October 1950

My earliest mental images are of the road trip my parents and I take in the summer of 1950. I am a little over three years old. We are driving the family car, our dark green Oldsmobile, across the country to New York City where we, car and all, will board the SS De Grasse, sailing to France for a reunion with my maman's family and friends.

I see myself riding in the back seat of the car on the way to New York smelling what I think is wool, probably my papa's army blanket, looking out the windows, tracings those decals on the side window. I remember sleeping on strange beds at the many auto courts we stay in, and Maman killing bugs we find crawling on the sheets. I listen to the sighing of cars passing in the night.

I stand on the back seat and stare at the man on the horse herding so many sheep that our car can't move.

During the night I watch as our car travels through a tunnel of tall pine trees filled with twinkling lights.

As we finally board the ocean liner, we all stare as our car seems to float over the ship then disappear into the cargo hold. The ocean liner takes seven days to arrive in Le Havre. Photographs taken on board show me in my father's arms at a Punch-and-Judy show, watching a kitten rather than the puppets, and one truly vivid memory: being vomited on by the steward delivering extra towels to our cabin during an ocean storm.

Saving for Good | 41

Once we arrive in Le Havre, we drive off in our Oldsmobile towards Maman's cousins' apartment in Paris. We will stay with them for almost three months. Lou Lou has a stiff left leg that swings out when he walks, and is thin with dark hair and stern looks. His wife Louisette is petite, round and always laughing. They are my godparents, and meet me for the first time. They have recently adopted a little girl, Catherine, about ten months younger than I. Maman's sister Mayie, husband Marcel Desclaux and their baby boy, Jean-Claude, join us arriving from Tizi Ouzou, Algeria. Marcel is in the French Foreign Legion.

A week later, Maman and Papa leave me in Paris with my godparents to visit Lucerne, Switzerland. Mayie, Marcel and their baby accompany them. They return a few days later during the night, coming to my bed, voices low, and a gloved hand places a small wind-up tin toy train near the headboard. I smile with my eyes closed. In the morning Catherine finds the train and crushes it. Lou Lou scolds Catherine and Maman reminds me that she is still a baby.

Later, sitting in the bathtub with Catherine, I watch as she releases little *crottes*, turds that float up to the surface. Transfixed, I forget about the broken train. What could be more interesting than floating turds?! I hear whispered adult conversations about my Aunt Mayie not bringing enough diapers for her baby, "How could she be so dirty?" There are other hushed conversations. I hear quiet words about a *cambrioleur*, a cat burglar, stealing across neighboring rooftops after dark. I feel for my round wooden truss that I wear across my belly button at night.

A giant birdcage takes me up and down in the building, a kaleidoscope of curlicue metal bars morphing as it moves. I am on a merry-go-round, up and down: the tin ring is always out of reach. A little gray-haired old lady dressed in a long black skirt leads my goat cart, round and round the park. Bunches of bright balloons sway in the wind, and a sound like a music box comes from the organ grinder. I drop a coin in the monkey's tin cup. Even for a three year old, Paris is magical, unforgettable.

As we drive to Biarritz we stop on the side of the road, surrounded by corn fields. We need to go to the bathroom. Maman opens the glove box and passes out toilet paper and we march into a row of corn. I'm not sure about peeing on the dirt, and it feels breezy on my bottom. But Papa says to hurry up before a bear licks my derrière!

We're at the beach. I'm sitting on the coarse warm sand of the Grand Plage, puzzling at the huge jagged rocks that look like dragons resting in the water. I can feel the grains sifting through my fingers while I play with a brightly painted wooden pail and shovel. It's time to leave and I'm told that I can't take the shovel and pail. But I want them so much.

Chapter 10:
Pasadena 1950 – 1955

We return to Pasadena in November 1950.

I am in nursery school, its nap time, and I lie down on a canvas cot supported by a wood frame. I see the teacher's thick legs walk by. The linoleum floor is made to look like the sides of alphabet blocks. I can't sleep. I can hear the teacher reading a story about an old woman with a toothache, whose kitten curls up on her jaw and soothes away her pain.

Monsieur Karlov, the grey-haired, strict dance master, leans on his cane and intones with a thick accent to my papa, "Save your money, Monsieur Aronoff!" He is referring to my lack of balance and balletic potential. I am only four. I love the costumes, and I am mesmerized by the blonde girl Yvonne, the serious 13 year old who dances on her toes. Nevertheless I am enrolled in the class, and I dance in a recital. But Monsieur Karlov is correct: I will never be a dancer. I topple over every time I try to stand in third position. Moving on, Maman enrolls me in ceramics class: this I can do.

Maman doesn't drive yet, so we walk, we take the bus. Sometimes we walk down the hill to visit my Kanka, my grandfather, my papa's papa. He lives in a little house near the fire station. We sit on metal chairs outside in the sunshine, peeking through the shade of the peeling trunks of giant eucalyptus trees.

Sometimes we go for Sunday rides. Papa drives the car and we take Kanka with us. Today we drive up the mountain near our house, Mt. Wilson. I like the smell of the sun-warmed dust and trees. I watch a tiny lizard dart through the fallen pine needles. Kanka watches, too, sharing my smile. On another Sunday we drive to Lake Arrowhead. It's also up on a mountain but it takes longer. I sleep but suddenly wake up, hearing a "thump, thump, thump," and Papa stops the car. Papa says that one of the tires is flat. While watching Papa change the tire I turn to look across the road and shade my eyes against the bright light reflecting off the water. We are at Lake Arrowhead.

Maman and me are in the basement of Woolworths in the housewares department. While my maman shops, I find some rainbow-hued clothes pins. I ask her if we can buy them and she says "No, we don't need them." When she looks away I take the packet and place it hidden in my apron pocket. Sometime after we arrive home, she discovers them and we walk back down the hill to the bus stop and return to Woolworths. There, she pushes me toward the sales clerk, forcing me to admit my theft and give back the brightly-colored clothes pins. I never steal again. But I never stop being attracted to brightly colored wooden items, either.

Whenever I don't feel good, Maman takes care of me in my bed, all day. I like it when she rubs my chest. She rubs it with Vick's and then carefully presses soft pale green paper, like very large toilet paper sheets, on top, so my pajamas don't get Vick's on them. Sometimes she gives me a *lavage*. I lie on my back atop a large towel that covers my bed and Maman places a peachy pink rubber hose in my bottom. She holds up a hot water bottle filled with warm soapy water and carefully fills me up. I like it. It's peaceful. If I get a tummy ache she gives me a spoonful of crunchy charcoal that's in a brown paper drum or sometimes she gives me a spoonful of bright green syrup that comes in a glass bottle. It smells like chewing gum.

My neck hurts, and it's cold. My hair's wet, hanging backwards in the bathroom sink. Maman is washing my hair. I don't want soap to get into my eyes. She uses a cup to rinse the bubbles out, and water drips down my back. My eyes are scrunched tight but I hear her say: *"Petits canetons, petits canetons"* "Little ducks, little ducks". She asks me if I can hear them splashing behind my head. *"Oui"*, I say with a giggle. Maman wraps a towel around my hair and I look like I'm wearing a giant snail shell, like the man on television who plays the organ (Korla Pandit, who is on just before "Time for Beany"). She also puts on big, gold rings on my ears. I stare at myself in the mirror. The tall *friction après le bain* bottle topped with a shiny black wooden knob sits on the bathroom counter next to me. The mirror has a different me.

We're going to a party at somebody else's house. Papa drives and Maman sits next to him. I am in the backseat. Papa's car is going backwards, parking. Maman turns around to look me over: she combs my hair, straightens my collar. If my eyebrows need smoothing, Maman licks her thumb and pats them down. I like her smell.

Sometimes I worry, about fire and other things. At night, shadows in my bedroom look like monsters and sometimes I dream about a little girl who skates on a frozen pond and watches darkness slowly covering the ice and her. Maman said she used to dream about taking care of a lot of little children during a storm, standing under a tree that is hit by lightning. I think mamans can get scared, too.

Today we go to the movies. Maman takes me. I've never been to the movies before. You sit on a padded chair in the dark with lots of other people. We watch "Snow White and the Seven Dwarfs". It is a cartoon, which I like very much. Except for the evil queen. When she turns into the old witch I jump down and go under my chair so I can't see her anymore. Maman has to pull me out. Now I am not sure I like the movies.

I wake up suddenly. My bed is moving back and forth. It's still dark outside. I call out to Papa to get out from under my mattress and stop shaking it. He comes into my bedroom laughing. How did he get out so fast from under my bed?? Papa says we had an earthquake. At breakfast I watch Maman carefully glue all the little pieces of the broken egg cup back together, then the dark blue candy dish and then she fixes the ceramic zebra's legs. They all fell down. I guess it was shaking in the kitchen and living room too. Papa is strong.

I am enrolled in San Rafael Elementary School. I am going to kindergarten. I love the two-story brick buildings with the gabled roof shaded by sycamores and eucalyptus. I meet "Dick and Jane" and a few girlfriends. We love to pretend we are wild horses running in herds outside during recess time. I want to be first but so does Donna. I feel mad that the others follow her so I push her face into the fountain as she drinks. She cries, tattles and I find myself sitting on a wooden bench outside of Dr. Michaels' office. He is the principal. I am in trouble. The big clock over his door ticks and I hear and smell the wet slap of the copying machine. My heart is pounding and I feel the fizz of worry in my stomach. The door opens and I enter his office. He is short and round and his blue suit fits him like a sausage skin. He wears a moustache and I know he is talking to me but I don't hear anything he says. From that moment on I am a "good girl" at school. But I never forget the feeling I have waiting outside Dr. Michaels' office that I am small and bad.

At school, outside time is much more interesting than inside. I smell the trees. Under the soles of my Keds, I feel the crunch of the decomposed granite. I skip, gallop, and hop Scotch. A boy scratches a big circle in the dirt with a twig and explains how to use pee-wees, boulders and cat's eyes to win at marbles. "Oomph!" Even the scary feeling of not being able to breathe as the tether ball smacks me in the stomach is exhilarating. My blisters have blisters: on my hands, behind my knees but still I hang and swing over and over the bar. I love it!

Papa trades the Olds for an army-green Morris Minor. It's a very small car compared to the big Oldsmobile. Since our home is at the top of a steep hill, Papa soon discovers he can't drive it up to the house unless he puts the car in reverse and drives backwards. Interesting and very funny, for me, but not Papa.

I hear a turning sound. Papa must be making something. He likes to build things, paint pictures and take my photograph. I go to the service porch door and see and smell my papa sweating. He's building a little brick house for Maman's new washing machine, the Bendix, right outside the service porch door. The turning sound is the cement mixer. Later I go with Papa to the hardware store to buy more cement mix. I wait by the counter and look at the things in the glass case and the posters on the wall. The clerk shows me a bird caller that sounds like a crow, another like a duck. I smile. But I don't say anything. I wish my papa would buy me a bird caller.

I can reach the light switch! I am getting bigger. And now I can go driving with my Kanka. He drives an old car that's dark green and smells like a wet wool blanket. I sit in the front seat, but I can't see out the windows unless I sit on my knees. No one can sit in the backseat. It's filled with junk. That's what Maman and Papa say. I like driving with Kanka because he always stops to see what's on the side of the road. And he always finds things: old furniture, newspapers, rugs, books. He parks the car and we get out to see what's good. He finds a bicycle wheel. Kanka throws it in the back seat.

Philippe lives down the street from me. He's a few months older than I am and his maman is a French war bride too. He has wavy light brown hair and when he smiles, his eyes crinkle into little grey triangles. Sometimes he comes over with his maman to visit. We play outside on the upper patio in the playhouse Papa built me. Today I am wearing my beaded Indian belt that spells "Lake Arrowhead". Our mamans are inside and Philippe and I take off our pants to look at each other's bodies. After a while they return and Maman notes that my belt is on upside down. I fix my belt. I know Maman knows what we were doing, but she says nothing. Another day when Philippe and I are walking by ourselves to kindergarten, I show him some pretend fruit that I made from colored modeling clay. Philippe teaches me that a lemon can't just be a round yellow ball because "there's a pointy part on each end," and he remolds my round yellow ball into a lemon shape. I learn from my experiences with Philippe that details matter.

It's late October and my papa and I go to school after dark for the Halloween carnival. I'm dressed up as a cat. It's exciting to be at school at night. There are so many people, it's really noisy, with so much laughing. At one booth someone glues black paper eyelashes on me. I am holding hands with my papa, shivering with excitement, when suddenly someone cracks an egg filled with confetti on top of my head. First I'm scared, then I'm delighted. It feels like magic.

When I'm about five and a half, I realize that I can read. And I can draw. I'm like a human duplicating machine. I might not be able to dance, but I can draw anything. Even my teacher asks me to show the class how to draw a dog, a horse, a grasshopper.

Maman takes me to visit Santa Claus. He is sitting in a sleigh outside of Bullock's department store in Pasadena. I am very excited to meet him. I've read about him in my "Babar's Noël" book. Inside there is a very detailed picture of his workshop. I tell Santa about all the toys I would like for Christmas. He's a good listener. At school I learn "Away in a Manger" and when Kanka calls on the telephone I sing it to him. He likes it but Papa thinks I shouldn't sing that song. When I draw a picture of the baby Jesus in the manger Papa argues with Maman about it. I don't understand why.

Maman teaches me many French songs. I like "*Au Clair de la Lune*" the best, and I can sing it to the very end. I also like "*Il est un Berger*" especially the "*ron, ron*" part. Sometimes I talk to Maman in her words, but most of the time I talk Papa's kind of words (English). I think I understand more French words than I can speak.

My brother Guy is born in February of 1953, the year I turn six. I am sitting in the little Morris Minor outside of Pasadena Huntington Hospital waiting for him to be born. I am in the front seat with my papa, watching him smoke Camels. He must be really distracted because when I ask him if I could try smoking his cigarette he lets me. I take a big drag and practically black out.

Maman wants a palm tree for the front yard and Papa knows how to get one – a full grown, big one! Part of downtown Los Angeles known as Bunker Hill is being torn down and if you can dig out and transport the trees, they're free. So on a very hot day, a big truck hauls our new tree up our steep hill and plants it right in the middle of our front lawn. Maman is very happy; me, not so much. I like real trees, the ones that have branches and lots of leaves. Oh, well.

Since my brother was born, not much has changed. He can't do anything. But I do like some of his toys, especially the painted wooden man whose arms and legs go up and down when you pull the string. My maman doesn't want me to touch it. I play alone in the bedroom. My brother's asleep in his bassinet, shadowed by a screen divider in our room. I can hear the radio; it's playing music from the "Coppelia" ballet. That's the music they always play before the program "Echoes and Encores" with Carl Princi. He talks on the radio. He has a nice voice and I like his last name.

Maman is busy doing something, so I go outside to play. "Gull darn it!" Papa yells. He must have wacked his thumb. He is in his workshop wearing his white undershirt with a V-neck. He's sweating. He puts down the hammer and picks up the saw. I watch his bottom lip go in and out. He is sawing some wood, and with each forward stroke he pushes his lip out. There's one little drip hanging from his nose. He wipes his face with his soft white handkerchief. I like his smell: wood shavings, sweat and talcum powder, all mixed up. Papa also likes to rest. Sometimes after he comes home from work or on weekends he lays down on the couch with the newspaper covering his face. I can wake him up and he doesn't mind. I love Papa's tight hugs and when he calls me *cocotte*.

I got my very own roll of Scotch tape and I am covering a folded piece of paper with the tape. I folded the paper in half and in half again and again and again until I couldn't fold it anymore. Then I covered it over and over with the Scotch Tape. The tiny shiny square goes in my pocket. Papa brought me home a small box of rhinestones from his work. I dug a hole in the backyard and buried it. It's buried treasure now.

Maman always reminds me to stand up straight, pull in my stomach and close my mouth. Papa thinks that a dump truck could make a U-turn in my mouth…

I examine Maman and Papa closely too. I notice that Maman has a tiny black dot on her front tooth and that sometimes she glues her right ear to the side of her head, and she has bumps on the sides of her big toes. Papa has a dent on the back of his head by his neck. (He says a toilet fell on it??) His third toe on his left foot crosses over his second toe and he has a little tiny piece of skin that sticks out of his hip. I think my maman is the most beautiful maman in the world and my papa is the most handsome, strongest papa.

I also like Superman, though. I watch him on television. He's not just strong, but he can fly. Sometimes I think I would like to be his daughter. I don't tell Papa this.

My papa works at a shoe factory and his uncle Philip is the boss. They make ladies' shoes. Sometimes I visit. It is very noisy and smells. It makes my eyes and nose itch. When you open the glass front door with the gold letters, the first thing you see is a low painted wood fence with a gate. Behind the fence are lots of ladies sitting at desks using shiny black machines. The machines have buttons with numbers on top and you use a handle on the side to make it work. The clickity-clack of the machines is loud, but inside the factory, through the double swinging doors where the shoes are made, is even louder and smellier too. And this room is big – bigger than any room I have ever seen. There are racks of wooden feet called "lasts," piles of leather, sewing machines, cutting machines and mountains of shoeboxes. And lots and lots of workers, ladies and men. The people who work there are very nice to me.

One day Papa brings me home a present from the shoe factory. It's not shoes, it's a Superman cape!! It's long and red with a big S sewn on. One of the stitchers at the factory made it for me. I love it and I tie it around my shoulders and race around the patio.

Some of my teeth in the front are getting very loose. Papa wants to tie a string around the really wiggly one on the top. He says he'll attach the other end of the string to the doorknob. I don't understand. Uh oh, now I understand! No! Ha! I run faster than the door slammed. Papa thinks it's funny. I do not.

The fruit bowl on the kitchen table is made out of a bumpy, milky white plastic that sits on a black metal stand with four little feet. The feet have tiny black rubber tips so they won't scratch the table. When I move the fruit bowl it sounds like an elephant's trumpet. It makes me smile. The fruit bowl usually holds red apples. My papa loves red apples. Whenever he eats one, he carefully peels it so that the skin spirals down in one unbroken curl.

Now that I can reach over the kitchen sink, I help him wash the dishes. He teaches me how to use my mouth to imitate a trumpet sound, and how to whistle. But I can't peel an apple like he can. (And never could.)

At night, after I'm in bed, the house is quiet. But I can hear the coyotes howling nearby, the crickets keeping time and the passing train. I feel Mitou jump on the bed, searching for the place to crawl under the covers. He sleeps between my legs. I sleep. Sometimes I dream I can fly.

There are always lots of animals: the owl that Maman finds sitting on her clothes line, the mountain lion that wanders into our service porch, the kingsnake Papa runs over with his car, on purpose. One day the postman brings the mail and with it, a bloody Maxwell House Coffee can. Inside an injured blue and yellow parakeet struggles to hang on. The postman found it on his route. Maman knows just what to do to make it better, and Romeo joins our family. Another day she finds a baby mouse that she puts in a shoebox and then in the oven. My eyes almost pop out of my head, but she explains she wants to keep the baby mouse warm, not cook it. We had a German shepherd, Duke, when I was two, but I don't remember him. Then we had Nina, a Cocker Spaniel, but she liked to eat out of the toilet so she moved away. Pitchounet is a small brown striped cat that finds our house and Maman and Papa decide that he can stay. Mitou doesn't really care about the new cat. Mitou, Pitchounet, and Romeo are our only real pets. One day Mitou walks in the house with a red slash across his back and Papa has to take him to the animal doctor for stitches. He places Mitou in the trunk to transport him but when we arrive at the animal hospital and open the trunk he's not there! Papa is speechless but then we hear a "meow" and Mitou pops out from the spare tire well. We both take a deep breath and smile.

My Kanka doesn't speak English very well (and he doesn't speak any French), but he teaches me how to communicate with cats. He pantomimes that you need to look at the cat's face and slowly blink your eyes and when the cat understands he will blink his eyes back at you. We practice with Mitou. Mitou understands! Then Kanka shows me tricks with a long piece of string. I carefully wind the string around my fingers in the certain pattern that he shows me, and finally I yank the string seemingly right through all my fingers. I stare at Kanka's eyes. One has a small yellow fleck on the white part. The colored circle parts make me think of my shiny black box of watercolors with the squares of muddled paint colors: I can see gray, brown, green. When he wears a sleeveless undershirt, I see the jagged scar that runs up his right upper arm. Some of his fingers have bumps on his baggy knuckles. When he laughs, he wheezes and sometimes he has to squeeze his rubber bulb inhaler. He calls me *"fegaleh"*, little bird.

I love my Kanka.

I look forward to laying down next to him on the redwood lounge, feeling the slow, baking drowsiness of the patio. Sometimes when it's too cold outside, Kanka and I play in the "rumpus" room, a big space under the main house. It has a long shadowy stairway. I carefully go down the steps: left foot, together, left foot, together. It's darker down here, and still chilly. "Kanka, where are you?" I see the dust drifting in the slant of sunlight coming from the high windows. There are the bookshelves, the brick wall covered with fishermen's nets, cork floats, shells. In the corner is the big blonde wood desk topped with a map of the world pressed under glass. The letter Maman is writing rests on the blotter and her fountain pen with the little arm on the side that sucks up ink, lays next to it. The letter paper is so thin that I can see the words written on the back and the front and sideways too. It looks like crisscross and I can't read it. In the middle of the room is the green Canasta table. Papa's paintings hang on the wall. I like the one that looks like a giant playing card, the Jack, the best. The scratchy floor matting tickles my bare feet. No Kanka. Maybe he's in the darkroom/bathroom under the stairs? But the red light is not on. Oops there he is, going *pipi*. What is that?! If that's his *kiki*, it's awfully dark and wrinkly, not like Guy's or Philippe's or Papa's.

I like helping Maman cook, especially when she's making chocolaty things or puffs. When she makes me hot cocoa Maman gives me the skin that forms on top of the milk when she cooks it. It tastes good. I also like licking the wooden spoon when she finishes making chocolate pudding, and eating the soft middle piece that Maman pulls out of the warm *pâte à choux*. She shows me how to take little spoonful's from the side of my bowl of farina so it's not too hot to eat. Sometimes Maman cooks the pointy part of a sewing needle but it's not for eating. She puts it in the flame on top of the stove until it glows and then takes out my splinters. I always get splinters. It doesn't hurt.

Today I had my picture taken at school. All the children from my class stood together in front our school. Even my teacher. The boys stood on wooden steps. Maman is disappointed that I didn't take off my jacket for the picture.

My brother Guy can sit up now and sometimes I can make him laugh. At breakfast, he sits in his highchair. There's a post between my chair and his and I play *"coucou"* (peek-a-boo) with him, popping out behind the post and surprising him. At first he looks like he's going to cry but then his eyes crinkle up and he giggles. It's so funny that I do it over and over again. Then he leans over and I lean over, touching our foreheads so close that his eyes blur into one large green and white marble. He usually smells pretty good, too. Like baby powder and Maman.

Whenever we come home from a drive downtown or visiting Maman's and Papa's friends, I can tell when we're getting close to our house. First we go through the four tunnels, then I see the white cross on the top of the hill, and then I see the neon sign with Barbara Ann's pretty face and sniff the warm yeasty smell coming from her bread factory. I like the drives we take, but I like the coming home better.

When I go outside to play on the upper patio I have to go under the trellis first. The trellis is covered with yellow roses. I hear loud humming. I look up, uh oh! The shiny black bumble bee is going to get me. I close my eyes and rush through. Safe! Go back again, no, no – yes, run back! The bumble bee will catch me! I love the bubbly feeling I get: I'm scared, but I'm brave. Today I decide that whenever I ride my tricycle and I hit my handlebars with something hard and it makes a loud noise, I could go deaf. (Deaf is when you can't hear anything. A boy in my class wears a hearing button in his ear with a wire that goes to a box that stays in his shirt pocket. He also wears glasses.) I hit my handlebars over and over again. I don't go deaf. There's other scary stuff in the patio: the oleander bush. Maman says it's poisonous and I should never eat the leaves. I could get very sick and die. I look at the flowers, though. They're pretty, but not as nice as the red hibiscus flowers. They are big and they're magic. At night the petals close, but in the morning they wake up and are beautiful again. There are spiders too. Maman says to blow gently and they'll walk away, never swat or squash.

Sometimes Kanka stays over for dinner. He thinks my maman is a good cook. He sits next to me. He always has a tiny glass of golden juice called whiskey. He pushes his glass in front of me and points to my thumb. He wants me to stick my thumb in the whiskey. I do and then I suck. It makes me scrunch my eyes and tickles my nose and throat and warms my tummy. Kanka points to the platter and Maman says, "Chicken". We are all eating and suddenly my Kanka is counting legs,

"*Eyn, tsvey, dray, FEER*!!" My papa starts laughing, but Kanka's mad at Maman. She cooked a rabbit, not a chicken. Uh oh.

I know Christmas is coming and I can't wait! Tonight Maman, Papa, Guy and I drive downtown to see in the decorated windows of all the big department stores. You can see tiny houses, people and animals and even snow, too. And a miniature train. I am so excited I'm almost jumping. Giant bells are attached to the street lamps with gold tinsel. It's wonderful.

Santa brought me my very own record player. It's oval shaped and made out of metal with pictures painted all around. And the circle that goes round and round where you put the record feels fuzzy. I got five records too, three red ones and two yellow. My favorite is "We're Building a City". I have to be careful plugging in the plug though. I could get shocked. (I'm not sure what that is but Papa said I wouldn't like it.) I sing with the records and I know almost all the words.

Today I got to help Maman take the decorations off the Christmas tree. Guy can't help because he puts everything in his mouth. There are lots of round balls that have a big dimple on one side, a very long silver prickly snake called a garland, and a star for the very top of the tree. The balls are very fragile. We have to take the wire hooks off each one. I can see my face in the silver balls. We wrap each ornament in tissue paper and put it in a box for next year because Christmas is over. Papa takes the dry tree outside to chop up and put in the incinerator. Christmas is better than my birthday.

Vacation is over and today I go back to school. Our class gets to go to the auditorium, but Dr. Michaels and our teacher tell us that Kathy, one of our classmates, is dead. Kathy is dead. I don't understand. Did she eat poison? How could this happen? What does that even mean that she's dead? Really? Will Kathy come back? Kathy has a thin left leg and wears a brace. She came to my birthday party. I play with her.

Dr. Michaels tells our class that she was killed by her papa when he set fire to their house on Christmas Eve. Only a visiting neighbor child and the family dog are okay. Kathy's brother, sister, maman and papa all died.

When I come home from school and tell Maman and Papa, they tell me that they already know and that they hid the Sunday Times so I couldn't see the pictures and find out. I am so sad and a little scared. I still don't understand. Papas are supposed to protect their families.

The milkman, the postman, the television repairman, the vacuum salesman, the Fuller Brush man, the encyclopedia salesman, the hobo, they all visit our house from time to time. Maman feeds the hobo. One day Maman and Papa decide to buy a set of red-orange leatherette books, ChildCraft. Maman puts the 12 volumes on the bookshelf that is my headboard. I like looking at the first two books, number one and two, poetry and fairy tales. But what I really like is thumbing through the booklet that came with the set. There's a picture of calendar pages all fanned out, flipping by. I think it shows time passing.

Sometimes at bedtime Maman reads to Guy and me. Our favorite story is "The Teeny Tiny Lady" (Volume Two). Maman is good at making the voices of the teeny tiny lady and the ghost. And every time she gets to the part that says, "Take it!!" Guy laughs and laughs and that makes me laugh even harder. Then Maman smothers our belly buttons with kisses, we screech and try to roll away from her tickling fingers and then she tells us to "*fais do do*".

Maman learns how to drive and we get another car. Its coral and white with four doors. I go with Maman when she grocery shops. We wait at the red light and I watch for the signal arm to go up and "say" go. When a streetcar goes by I can see sparks fly off the wires on top. At Ralphs grocery store we stand in line waiting for our turn to pay. I notice candy bars. I ask to have one but Maman says "No." I persist, but she will not change her mind. I start to whine and Maman takes my hand and we leave Ralphs and all our groceries. Maman talks in French to me when she's mad. She talks in French a lot. Another time we are in the dressing room at Bullock's. It's not much fun but then I discover that the three mirrors move, they have hinges. If I position them just so I can see gazillions of me, over and over again, getting smaller and smaller. No matter how long I look there's still more me's. I like looking at each me, even the little ones.

Sometimes we go to Vroman's bookstore to pick up books that Papa ordered. One time when Maman was paying for Papa's books the lady wrote down Maman's name. Maman wasn't happy about that. She said that some people don't like the books that Papa reads. I don't understand. (Later I would learn that these were left-wing political books. This was during the McCarthy era.)

Maman reads books too, but she gets her books in the mail, from her cousins in France. She has to use a knife to separate the pages. She always puts leaves or flowers inside to save her place.

I make my own books. I draw the pictures that "tell" the story and then I make the cover out of the cardboard that comes inside my papa's folded laundry shirts. Papa takes my book to the shoe factory and the workers put "eyelets" on the left side. (Eyelets are metal holes that shoe laces go through.) I tie a shoe lace through the holes and then my book is finished and ready to read. Maman and Papa like my first book. It's about a mouse family. There's a maman mouse and papa mouse and an older sister mouse and soon, a baby mouse. The sister mouse gets in trouble and gets a spanking.

While I'm in school my brother locks Maman out of the house and he is still inside! She goes to the neighbor's house and calls Papa to come home and unlock the door! Silly Guy. I don't think Maman is very happy with Guy.

My second grade class is going on a field trip today. Guess where? We get to ride on a big yellow school bus to my papa's work! I'm so excited but when my teacher, Miss Patrick, asks me to introduce my papa to the class I run to Bert who is a salesman and not my papa. Bert, Papa, and my teacher are surprised. I am too excited. I feel proud but shy all at the same time and now I am embarrassed. Sometimes I don't understand me.

Today at school we all got to march into the auditorium holding flags. I love the music. The teacher said it was Sousa. I'm not sure what that means but it made shivers down my back and I felt important. We made our own flags out of red, white and blue paper. We have a real big one in our class that hangs in the corner. Every morning we say the pledge to it. I am not sure what that is, but Papa got upset about the "under God" part. Sometimes he mixes me up.

Chapter 11:
The Move 1955

One day in the beginning of the new year I hear Maman and Papa talking about moving. I'm not sure what that means. They talk a lot about the smog too, and they don't like it. Smog is when I can't see across the street and when I breathe deep I can feel the "tight" in the bottom of my chest. Papa says that you used to be able to see the ocean from our front yard. Maman sometimes says she's bored too but I am not sure what bored means, either.

I like my school and my friends. I like exploring at the end of my street where there are no houses and the weeds are so tall you can hide. My friend Timmy and I like to go there. Way below us is the speedway, and on the other side is the giant rock with an eagle shape on the top. It's huge. On some days, a warm wind blows so hard, sand prickles our faces. We have to scrunch our eyes and cover our noses. Our hair stands up. Today we find a broken watch in the rocky, scrubby hillside. We work hard and when I get home for dinner I find little brown dirt balls between my fingers when I wash my hands.

A house is being built across the street on one of the empty lots. A family moves in before it's finished. There are three blond boys and a mom and a dad. I think the biggest boy is younger than me. I am almost eight. They are always barefoot and never wear shirts or undershirts even on real cold days and there are bed sheets covering their windows. There's dust everywhere because there is no grass or plants, just dirt. All the boys have a big circle shaped scar that goes around their belly buttons. I don't play with them and I don't think they go to school. And Maman doesn't like them.

It's Sunday and we are going out for our drive: the whole family, even our new dog Kim. (Timmy's boxer dog had puppies and we bought one.) "Kimmie", that's what I call Kim, reminds me of Guy: he puts everything in his mouth and runs fast. And he's so cute and soft. He's the color of caramel candy. Maman took him to the animal doctor to get his ears and tail cut! They are all bandaged with white tape. I don't think he minds because he's still chewing and running.

If it's nice we go to the beach. Today we went to the palisades overlooking Santa Monica beach. While we took pictures, Maman heard some people speaking French. They're older, a man and woman, and Maman introduced herself and tomorrow she is going with them to Burbank to visit the Walt Disney Studios and meet Walt Disney! He made the "Snow White" movie and he has a show on television. Children can't go.

Sometimes on Sunday we visit Uncles Philip, Charlie and Morris and Aunt Pauline at their mansion in Hancock Park on Hudson Avenue. They are Kanka's brothers and sister, and they all live together. Maman calls Kanka's brothers *les oeufs cuit*, the "hard boiled eggs". I call them the "little people" because they're so short. Kanka is not little, though. He's the same size as Maman and Papa. But all the brothers and the sister sound the same when they talk, and they all wheeze when they laugh. (Great Aunt Pauline doesn't laugh much though.) There's another sister, Pearl, but she doesn't live with the "little people". I think I met her once. She's also short. There was another sister, Clara, but she died when I was a little girl and I don't remember her.

Kanka has a daughter, Papa's sister. Her name is Ruth. She has a boy named Gerald who is younger than me. She's my aunt, but I don't like talking to her. I get quiet with her. I don't like talking with Papa's Aunt Pauline, either, especially when she has on her fur shawl with the fox heads on one side and tails on the other. I think Kanka gets mad at Ruth and Pauline. Sometimes I hear Maman and Papa talking about them. It's not happy talk. They say that Ruth and Pauline are "miserable" people and always complain.

Anyway, lately we've been looking at houses. I'm beginning to understand what moving might be about. We visit a pretty neighborhood with windy streets shaded by big leafy trees. We don't stop. But one Sunday we visit a house in Los Angeles on Alvira Street. The street is flat and all the houses look alike with red tile roofs. All the trees on the street are palm trees. We go inside. It smells funny. The grown-ups all talk, but I don't listen.

I missed school today because Maman is so sick she stays in bed all day. She has bad diarrhea. I take care of Guy. The next day Maman feels better but now she's worried about Guy because he isn't walking so good. One of his knees is shaky. She thinks he might have polio. That's what my dead friend Kathy had. I hope not. Two days later the doctor says Guy is okay.

My friend Margaret is turning eight years old and I am invited to her birthday party. She has a real swimming pool so we can bring our bathing suits. But it's April and it rains, so we can't go swimming. Upstairs, we stand at her bedroom window and look down at the pouring rain making circles in the pool. I'm not disappointed though, because she gives each one of us a small wooden figurine, painted with bright colors. I love touching it.

Maman is busy cleaning our house, scrubbing the navy blue linoleum floor in the kitchen. Ernie, Papa's friend, helps her. His skin is the color of dark chocolate and he's very nice. Sometimes he stays for dinner.

Now it's my turn to be eight. I invite 10 friends and my second grade teacher, Miss Patrick, to my house for a party after school. Everyone comes. Guy cries the whole time. I don't like my presents much: clothes and books. But Maman and Papa get me a two-wheeler bike. I can't ride it without the training wheels and I can't go on the sidewalk. It's too hilly here. So I ride in tight circles on the upper patio. Kanka brings me a gold ring with an emerald in the middle. It's my birthstone, and it's green. His birthday was a few days before, and we gave him a bottle of whiskey and I drew him a picture too.

I like having birthdays except for one thing: I have to go for a "check-up" at Dr. Goldman's. I always get a bubbly feeling in my tummy when we go. We drive on the speedway and then to Sixth Street to Beverly Hills. His office is on Robertson Boulevard. When you go inside you have to wait your turn to see the doctor. The waiting place has a big aquarium full of fish, but what I look at are the doorknobs. The doorknobs are near the tops of the doors. Only the adults can reach that high.

Finally it's my turn. Maman and me walk into the examining room. I don't like the smell. It smells like shots, and it's also cold. I have to take off all my clothes except my panties. Dr. Goldman comes in. He's big and bald and he smiles. He wears a long white coat and talks mostly to Maman. He checks my body and then takes me to get X-rays. I walk down the hall in my bare feet. It's cold. I go into a dark room and stand against the glass. It's so cold. Soon it's finished. It doesn't hurt.

But when I go back into the examining room Maman says I'm going to get a shot. I start to cry but she says if I'm brave we can get a real turtle! The nurse comes in and gives me the shot in my bottom. I don't cry. But I wonder why Dr. Goldman never gives the shots. I get dressed and we walk down the hall to his office. We sit down in front of his desk and he talks with Maman. I don't listen. Instead I examine the big circus mural behind Dr. Goldman and think about turtles.

Later we go to the Farmer's Market. It's close to the doctor's office. It's a busy place full of fruit and vegetable stands; all kinds of different eating places that you can sit and eat at little tables outside; and some small stores that sell baskets, candy, magic tricks and a pet shop. There are lots of trees so the sunlight speckles the ground like lace. We go inside the pet shop and Maman buys me a small turtle and a clear plastic pool, complete with a tiny island and palm tree. And an orange box of turtle food. I name him Snooper. He's my best birthday present!

It's warm and bright, I'm waiting outside in the front yard. Papa asked me to stay outside. I hear Maman crying, screaming in pain. Papa is trying to help her. Her back has been hurting and today it's worse. They decided to put a giant Band-Aid on her back to try and make it feel better. But it doesn't work and now it hurts so much to peel it off. I can't stand it. I cover my ears. I don't want to hear my maman cry. Make it stop! I want her hurting to go away now and not ever come back. I will give her my turtle.

June: Today Guy got baptized. A man called a priest, dressed in a black robe with a fancy blouse, said some special words over Guy's head, and put some oil and holy water on his forehead. Guy was being silly: he asked for more holy water. Then, while Maman was holding him over her shoulder, he reached the light switch and everything went dark in the church! Anyway, Guy's now Catholic. I was baptized too, a long time ago, but I don't remember anything about it. Except I'm Catholic, I think.

Maman is very busy with Guy. He runs pretty fast now and still puts everything in his mouth, especially his thumb. Today he got stung by a bee on his thumb. Then he put his thumb in his mouth and got stung on his tongue. Poor Guy. Maman called the doctor. Then again this week, Guy began choking at the kitchen table. Maman thought he might have swallowed a little wire, so she rushed him to the doctor's. They took an X-ray but didn't see any wire.

This time Guy got into all of Maman and Papa's pills. He swallowed lots and Maman called the doctor and he told her to make Guy throw up. She did and he did. They didn't have to go to Dr. Goldman but Maman is not happy.

Tonight after dinner, Guy escaped out the front door and ran down the street. Maman and Papa don't notice right away, and Papa has to use the car to find him. They are scared and mad and glad when they find him. I knew he would be back.

School is over for the summer and I will be a third grader next September. That means I can play in the lower terrace for recess. And I'll be old enough to join the Bluebirds, part of the Camp Fire Girls, when I come back to school. All my girlfriends are going to join too. Last week, Maman and I went to a meeting about joining. I'm so excited because we will all get to wear blue uniforms and go to meetings after school and go camping too! Oh, my hair is growing and I can almost put it in a ponytail! (I've always wanted a ponytail just like Donna's.) And Maman and Papa are now Mommy and Daddy. That's how all my friends call their mommies and daddies, even Phillipe. So I am too.

I am taking swimming lessons two times a week. Mommy drives me to the pool and she and Guy watch me from the benches. I want to swim but I can't do it very well. The pool is full of children and teachers but no one is from my class. So much noise and splashing. I don't like the water rushing up my nose and the inner tube hurts under my arms. And the water burns my eyes and smells funny. Finally I can do the dog paddle but I am still sinking a lot.

Our house is "for sale." That means some other family will give Daddy money to buy our house, then they will move into our house and we have to move out. Mommy is always cleaning and telling Daddy that no one wants to buy our house. She doesn't like that. But one day a man and a woman visit and decide to buy our house. We're moving to the house on Alvira Street in Los Angeles. I don't want to move. I want to stay here but I don't tell Mommy and Daddy. It's too late anyway. I will miss all my friends, my teachers, my school, my house, my bedroom and becoming a Bluebird. I am not happy.

We visit the "new" house again. The older girl who lives there is nice. She shows me her bedroom. I guess it will be Guy's and my new bedroom. It has a dressing room with a mirror hanging over a built-in desk, a closet you can walk inside with a built-in toy box, and two entry doors, one near the bathroom and another close to the front door of the house. It's nice, but the whole house still smells funny, sort of like the damp wool smell of Kanka's car. The girl also gives me a big box of her old books: "Beverly Gray Mysteries;" "Cherry Ames, Junior Nurse;" "Nancy Drew," and many more. She says she's going to college. I don't know what that is and I don't ask.

On August 5th, a big truck comes to move all our furniture and things to the new house. After the truck leaves, standing in the kitchen, I think my house looks naked, lonely and it sounds echo-y. I notice the kitchen doorframe and see all the marks Mommy and Daddy made on each of my birthdays, showing how much I had grown. I guess we can't take that. Anyway, Mommy worked all day scrubbing the kitchen floor to make it nice and clean for the new people. Later she says that, right after we left, the new people tore out our blue linoleum kitchen floor. She is mad. I wish she wasn't mad but I know she worked so hard that her back hurts again.

I am lying in my old bed in our new bedroom trying to fall asleep. I can see the full moon peeking through one of the windows, and all the parts of the room slowly appear. I stare at the ceiling. It looks like it's decorated with cake frosting and in the middle it looks like there's an upside down fruit bowl. It's the light fixture. My eyes look down and follow the pattern of the wood floor into the dark nubby rug over to Guy's crib. The night sounds are different. No howling coyotes, but I can hear the next-door neighbors talking inside their house, the furnace groan and parts of the floor creak. Scorched dust drifts out of the vents. Mitou doesn't come to my bed. When I wake up I see the sunlight streaming through pink curtains sprinkled with little white bumpy dots. I think I am going to take Mommy's little lavender-filled basket and put it between my sheets.

I'm still not sure about the new house. The backyard is a big flat square with a playhouse. I liked the playhouse Daddy made better. We left it in Pasadena. There's an incinerator in the back corner of the yard and a small garage on the other side. A big clothesline with rusty posts goes through the middle. There are houses on both sides and behind too and you can look into all the neighbors' backyards. And the streets are so straight, no ups and downs but there are little trucks that visit our street almost every day. One truck whistles a "whoot whoot" and the other has bells. That's the signal for everyone to come out and buy donuts, bread or ice cream. Mommy says we don't need to buy any because she makes better desserts. She does.

Our furniture looks different in the rooms, like they don't really match. But in the service porch there's a door that opens into a "pantry." A pantry is a place to put canned food and stuff but the surprise is the floor. The floor is really a door that opens up to stairs that go down to a basement. A basement is where the furnace hides and where you can hang laundry when it's raining outside. There are some rough wood shelves and you can see the dirt under the house but it's not a rumpus room. I hope Kanka will visit us at our new house. I haven't seen him in a long time.

I like our new kitchen though. It has a "breakfast room," which is different than a dining room. I'm sitting at the kitchen table, staring at my reflection in the silver teakettle. My face looks all fat like in a fun house mirror, big brown eyes, pig nose, making faces, and tiny teeth smiling. See, Mommy just walked past. She's getting dinner ready. She's lighting the oven with a match. KA BOOM! There is a flash and a bang. Whoa that's a surprise! But Mommy's laughing. She looks funny with only one eyebrow.

Another thing that's different from our house in Pasadena is when you walk through the front door, there's a foyer. That's a little room with six sides and each side has a doorway leading to another room. The first side is the front door and then to the right is the entrance to the living room and you have to step down. The next side is a door to our bedroom. Straight ahead is the hallway where the blond desk that used to be in the rumpus room sits. Above the desk in the ceiling is a stained glass window that lets in sunlight, making colored shadows. The next side is the entrance to the dining room. And the last door is to the coat closet, just left of the front door. But we don't keep coats inside. Instead there's a pile of Daddy's Time magazines stacked on the floor, Mommy's big silky plaid umbrella with the brown leather handle, my shiny white ballet tutu from when I was little and Mommy's dark blue cloak from when she used to be a nurse. There's a hole in it, that she said came from a bullet. Hanging high above the foyer is a fancy light, called a chandelier.

Today Daddy, Uncle Philip and I are going to a new amusement park named Disneyland. It takes a long time to drive there, and we pass lots of orange groves. I watch from the car window as they fan by. Disneyland just opened and Uncle Philip has a shoe store on the Main Street inside the park. Mommy can't go with us because she can't get a babysitter for Guy. It's a very interesting big place but it's too hot. A man with a large camera is following us and taking our picture. We bring back a French bread that is shaped like a crocodile for Mommy. It was a long day.

Daddy and Uncle Philip at Disneyland, Summer 1955

I make new friends, Sue, Harold and Carole. They are all eight or almost eight years old, and they all live on Alvira Street. I discover that everyone is Jewish. Almost all my friends in Pasadena were Presbyterians and they told me that Jewish people had killed Jesus so I never told them that my daddy was Jewish. I think Daddy was born Jewish, like his family. But I think he isn't anything now, except maybe Communist? He never talks about religion except that time I drew pictures of Baby Jesus and sang Kanka Christmas carols. He didn't like it. But Kanka did.

Just like Guy, I was baptized but I'm not really sure what I am. But my mommy is for-sure Catholic. I go to church with her twice a year, at Easter and Christmas. She taught me how to pray and cross myself and kiss my fingertips. Every night I pray to God to take care of my family, my friends and my animals. To keep me safe, Mommy put between my mattresses a flat silky pillow with a sacred heart embroidered on it. I also avoid stepping on cracks on the sidewalk. My godparents gave me a special gold medallion with Mary's (Jesus' Mommy) face, and I always wear it around my neck tucked under my undershirt. Now that I live on Alvira Street I still don't know "what" I am, though. Why does everyone have to be only one thing?

I did hear Mommy and Daddy arguing about my new school. Mommy wants me to go to a Catholic school. Daddy said "No!"

I will start my new school, Carthay Center, soon. It's not a Catholic school, it's a regular school. Mommy takes me to the Attendance Office to enroll me and we meet the Principal, Mrs. Troeger. She's tall like Mommy. I am very quiet, a little shy and kind of scared. But she isn't anything like Dr. Michaels. I think that's a good thing. The school doesn't look like San Rafael. It has a tile roof and it's a lot bigger especially the playground. But there are no upper and lower terraces and no big trees. I will be in the "B3," my teacher will be Mrs. Saunders and my classroom will be in a bungalow. I'm not sure what a bungalow is. Maybe that's the "B" in B3. I think that's the third grade but I don't ask. I miss my old school and friends already.

Mommy takes me shopping for my school clothes. We go to Bullock's Westwood, not Pasadena. After we buy new dresses, two plaid skirts (with pleats that look like my toy accordion) and socks, we go upstairs to get my hair cut. I ask Mommy to just have my bangs trimmed but she says "No" – I need to have a proper haircut for school, no ponytails. I am disappointed and a little mad. But I get to sit on a pretend horse while my hair gets cut. Later we go to the shoe store to buy new school shoes. (Daddy's shoe factory only makes ladies shoes so we have to buy children shoes.) I slide my feet wearing the new shoes into the bottom of a big machine that X-rays my feet to see if they are the right size. I can see my bones. Strange.

Mommy signed me up at the Westside Jewish Center for more swimming lessons. I arrive for my lesson and when I am given my towel and locker assignment the young woman at the desk reminds me that I can't wear jewelry in the pool, pointing to my necklace. Mommy wants to keep it for me but I insist that I'll put in my plaid bag with my clothes in the locker. I don't want that young woman to look at my Mary necklace too closely. I'm not taking any chances.

Later, after I get out of the pool and start to dress I can't find the necklace! It isn't in the bag! I search in the locker, on the floor but I can't find it!! Mommy is very upset that I have lost it and takes me to the Lost and Found office at the Jewish Center and describes to the young man EXACTLY what my necklace looks like. Oh God I want to run away and hide… (And no one ever turns in my Mary necklace, either.)

Anyway, I finally learn to swim and it's a good thing too because it's been so hot. I don't know if it's hot in Pasadena but in our new neighborhood it's awful. It's been 110 degrees. Even Daddy didn't go to work today and instead we went to the beach. We took Kimmie the dog too. Mitou and Pitchounet stayed hidden in the garage. Tomorrow we might go to Uncle Philip's mansion on Hudson Avenue. They have a big pool and a cabaña. It will be cooler there.

Today I started my new school. I walked and used the "underpass" to cross the street. It's a people tunnel under Olympic Boulevard. And I found out what a bungalow is. It's a small building not attached to the real school. It's only one classroom. My teacher is nice. She's short and round and her son is also a B3. (And 'B3' means the first part of the third grade; 'A3' is the second part.) All the kids in my class already know how to multiply. I'm not sure what "multiply" means. We get sheets of paper that have "problems" on them. I don't understand.

A new friend, Harriet, comes to the rescue. She shows me how to get the answer: a magical plastic pencil box! It has this little white piece that slides across the top of the box and the number that shows through the little hole is the answer. That's how you multiply, I guess. Anyway, Harriet tells me that you have to go to the market to buy one. All the kids have one. I've got to ask Mommy and Daddy. Carthay Center School is a lot different than San Rafael.

Instead of going home for lunch I bring a lunch box and thermos. I eat with Harriet on the benches outside of our classroom. My lunches don't look like hers. I wish I had a tuna fish sandwich or a peanut butter and jelly. Mommy packs me leftovers of dinner, chicken legs, vegetables and fruits, things like that. And I drop my thermos a lot. I ask Mommy to make me a sandwich for lunch just like the other kids. Next day at lunch I open my box and find a sandwich! I am so excited until I unwrap the wax paper and bite in. Mommy made a cream cheese and grated bittersweet chocolate sandwich. Harriet wants to trade. Okay that works.

Tonight is "Back to School" night. I am taking Daddy to visit my new school and my classroom. I remind him while we're walking in the underpass that "they" (my teacher and the principal) think I'm a good girl and not to tell them what I'm really like. Daddy smiles and promises he won't say a word.

Mommy signs up Guy to go to nursery school. He used to go to a nursery school before in Pasadena once a week. He likes it at first but after a week he starts to cry. And he's getting sick again. He gets colds all the time and he doesn't like to eat. Mommy says he's cranky and whines a lot. Less than a month later, he stops going to the Westside Nursery School.

Mommy is cranky and whines a lot too. She is always waiting for letters from France and she doesn't feel good a lot. She has headaches, tummy and backaches, gets tired and her leg hurts her. And Daddy had to go to another shoe show, this time in Chicago. Mommy misses him a lot when he doesn't come home for dinner. And Mommy is mad at Kimmie because he peed so much on the new little tree she planted in the backyard that it died. Then he ripped one of my party dresses off the clothesline and ate it and then got sick and threw up all the pieces. She says she wants to give him away. And she says she's bored again.

Guy escaped today while Mommy was on the telephone. The postman found him a block up the street and brought him back. I think Mommy is frustrated with Guy. I think that's the right word. She says: "*Il est infernal, fait bêtises sur bêtises.*" ("He is infuriating, doing silly things on top of silly things.") That's French. Sometimes she calls me a good-for-nothing, a "*vaurienne*".

Daddy flew to another shoe show, this time in Seattle, and Mommy is really upset. Five days later, he's back home and he brought Mommy a new purse and me and Guy little wooden push puppets. Mine is a dog and I love it! Guy already broke his and I am hiding mine...

Our next-door neighbor on my bedroom side had a fight with Mommy today. She said our incinerator smells bad. She always complains about something: Kimmie barking, Guy and I being too noisy. Mommy says she's a "*sorcière*" (witch) and "too bad."

It's Christmas vacation, so I don't have any school. Today Mommy let me babysit Guy all by myself. He slept the whole time. She went to the dentist. It's getting close to Christmas day, and I can't wait. I don't really believe in Santa anymore, though. I waited in the fireplace last year and I never saw him. Anyway Mommy was happy today because she got to talk to her cousins in France, my godparents Lou Lou and Louisette. She called them on the telephone. Mommy sometimes cries when she's happy.

On Christmas morning we opened our presents. From Mommy and Daddy, I got a doll stroller and a Brownie camera with a roll of film. From my godparents, some books written in French. From Kanka, a new record player with three speeds with a lid that turns it into a little suitcase. I don't see him too much anymore, I miss him.

Daddy's army buddy, Freddy Horton, came over for turkey dinner later. He made Mommy cry when he showed her pictures that he took when he went to France last month. I think she was happy and sad. She said, "*Je pleure comme une Madeleine.*"

Chapter 12:
Home Sick 1956

It's the New Year and there's no school. Today our family went to a merry-go-round not too far from our house. Mommy banged her head on the door frame getting out and decided to stay in the car.

Christmas vacation is over and I get to go back to school. I like this school better now. But my swimming classes start again and now Mommy signed me up for fencing classes too. I don't like taking these classes so much because I don't know anyone. There's no one from my school or from Alvira Street. And it's at the Jewish Center, which I still worry about.

It's been raining for over a week and we have "rainy day schedule." That means that we don't have recess outside. We eat snacks and lunch in our classroom and have to play "Head's Up Seven Up." Everybody seems to know the game, but I never heard of it. Today it rained so much that Mommy had to pick me up early from school in the car, and school will be closed tomorrow because of the flooding.

At home, I look up at the stained glass skylight in the hall ceiling watching the rain fall. The colors blur into a hundred pieces, running off in all directions. From one moment to the next, the glass shines, then dims. The shadows cover my body. I wish I could catch all those colors, hold them tight, and stop them from disappearing through my fingers.

It's February 3rd, Guy's third birthday, his "golden" birthday. My "golden" birthday won't come until I will be old: 31 years old! And it's also Guy's three-year-old check-up at Dr. Goldman's. I am going too, but I don't need to be checked. When we climb into the car to go,

Mommy accidently smashes Guy's finger with the car door! He cries so hard he can't make any noise. Mommy drives right away to the doctor's office. They x-ray his right pointer finger and the doctor says the bone looks like sand! Mommy is very upset. Now Guy has a cast on his finger. He wants his diaper *doudou* (blankie) to hold and he is very sad and scared. He got shots, too. Poor Guy.

After dinner we walk up Alvira Street to the record store on Pico Boulevard. We are going to buy some phonograph records. Mommy chooses Harry Belafonte's "Calypso." It's a long-playing record. It plays on a slower speed, 33 rpm. Instead of three or four records in an album book, there's only one big black disk that comes in a big square cardboard envelope with Harry's smiling face on it. Mommy also picked out a 45 rpm record (it's a smaller disk with a bigger hole) of "Greensleeves" and I got to pick one too: Elvis Presley's "Hound Dog" ("Love Me Tender" is on the back). I saw him sing on the Ed Sullivan Show. That's on television, on Sunday nights. He's cute, sort of. Elvis, not Ed.

On Pico Boulevard, we can find nearly everything we need to buy. There's Fox Big Town Market, the 5 & 10 & 25 Cent Store, the bowling alley, the Picfair Theater and the record store. I especially like the 5 & 10 & 25 Cent Store. It reminds me a little of Woolworth's in Pasadena except there's no downstairs and we don't have to drive. I like to browse. There are lots of glass cases with things to buy: red rolls of caps for toy guns, small painted tin cars, straw Chinese finger pulls, boxes of model airplanes, tiny pink plastic babies and other stuff for grown-ups.

If you keep walking on Pico, you will come to La Cienega Boulevard. Just around the corner there is a newspaper and magazine stand. A very short man who wears a dirty baseball cap yells out in a singsong voice that there are newspapers to buy. And if you walk a little farther, there's an ice cream store with 31 different flavors!

Pitchounet is lost. I can't find him. He didn't come home again for dinner tonight. Daddy reminded me that it's almost spring so maybe Pitchounet is looking for a girlfriend. Why would a cat need a girlfriend?

It's been almost two weeks and he still hasn't come home. On Friday Daddy found his body near the incinerator. Daddy wouldn't let me look at him. I feel so sad and wonder what happened. I wonder if Mitou misses him.

It's "Open House" again at school and this time I go with Mommy. It's kind of fun to show her my desk, my folder and my work on the bulletin board. I felt a little silly and shy with Mommy but proud too because Mommy is the most beautiful of all the mommies. And my teacher tells her that I'm "an excellent student."

I don't think I'm "excellent" at home though. I don't like to eat much and when we eat dinner Kimmie always sits next to me because when I wipe my mouth with my napkin I secretly put my chewed up food in it. Then I put my napkin on my lap and slowly move it to the side and let Kimmie eat my food. Mommy and Daddy don't notice. Today Mommy and Daddy argued about me at breakfast. I didn't want to finish my orange juice. Daddy said I had to and Mommy said I didn't. I feel bad that I made them argue.

I "talked back" today and Daddy gave me a spanking on my *derrière*. I wanted to watch Elvis on The Milton Berle Show but Daddy said it's a school night. I said "So what" and made a face. Mommy and Daddy didn't argue about me today. They agreed that I was "insolent".

Tonight at dinner I asked Daddy about a new word I learned at school: fuck. Daddy put his fork down and said that it's a word that boys should never say and that girls should never think it. But he never told me what it meant and Mommy didn't say anything either. Guy wasn't listening. I think it's got something to do with *kikis*, penises. At recess, some of the boys were laughing and making an "O" with their thumb and pointer finger on one hand and using their pointer finger from their other hand to poke in the "O" and saying "fuck". Weird. Oh well. I'll ask Harriet.

I turned nine years old and had my friends Harold, Harriet, Richard, Carole and Sue come to my house for my party. Kanka gave Daddy money to buy me a new bike. (My legs are too long for my old one, my knees hit the handlebars.) And Mommy and Daddy gave me a blimp ride! At first I didn't understand, then they explained: a blimp is like a giant balloon shaped like a football that slowly flies high in the sky. And underneath, attached to the blimp, is a little room for the passengers. There's a driver too.

Daddy drove us (Daddy, Mommy, Guy and I) to a big grassy field where the blimp was parked. We didn't have to wait long. Only three or four other people rode with us. But when we sat down, we had to yell really loud to talk because it has a very noisy motor. It was exciting to be up so high. When I looked out the windows, the people looked like little ants and the cars looked like toys! I still dream about flying free like a bird. This was close.

Mommy voted for the first time today. She voted for Adlai Stevenson and he won! He wants to be the next President of the United States of America but the run-off won't be until the fall. President Eisenhower wants to have a longer turn being the president. He is a Republican and plays golf. Mommy and Daddy are Democrats and so is Adlai. Not sure what that means but I can't vote anyway except at school. And, guess what? School is over for the summer! I am excited and a little sad. I really like school and my friends now, but I will like being able to play all day too.

Our family is going on vacation for almost two weeks and Mitou and Kimmie are going to stay at the veterinarian's. Romeo and Snooper are staying with Harold next door. We're all packed and ready to go. We're taking Mommy's car because we can't all fit into Daddy's Morris. Guy and I sit in the back seat. Daddy has to fill up the tank first because it's going to be a long drive. The car rolls over the wire that 'ding-dings' for the filling station attendant and I can already smell the gasoline. I love the smell. Daddy tells the man to fill it up with ethyl. And Mommy asks for the S&H Green Stamps while another attendant cleans the car windows. I look at the sign with the big numbers, 23.9¢ and the big red flying horse. Finally the tank is filled, Mommy got her stamps and Daddy starts the car. We're off.

On our way to La Jolla, the man on the radio said that two passenger airplanes collided over the Grand Canyon. Collided means crashed into each other. Everyone died. I can't stop thinking about the passengers. There must have been some children like me and Guy on their vacation, probably looking out of the windows, flying through the clouds like birds, and then it wasn't - everything burning and falling. I have to stop thinking about it.

We are staying at a motel near the sand so we can walk to the beach every day. We dig for sand crabs, find tiny seashells and sand dollars, and dig lots of big holes. But mostly I just watch the waves and birds flying overhead.

Today we visited a place called Mexico. It's a different country you can drive to and the people don't speak English or French. They speak Spanish. Little barefoot children yell, "*Esta chicle!*" I don't like it too much. There were flies everywhere, even inside the glass cases of the bakery shop. We went to Rosarito Beach to see the ocean. They have horses you can ride on the sand. We didn't ride but just watched. Mommy was sad for the horses. They had flies all over their eyes, biting. She took out her handkerchief and cleaned off all their faces.

On the way back home we stopped at a mission. It's sort of like a church but it's very old. This mission has lots of pigeons. Daddy bought me some breadcrumbs to feed them, and they flew all over me

and Daddy, on our heads, our shoulders and our arms. But when they flew away, Daddy's brown suit was all covered in bird kaka! Not me though. Daddy was mad and laughing at the same time. Mommy took pictures.

It was fun to take a vacation but I'm glad that we're home. Home. I didn't think of Pasadena first this time, I thought of our house here on Alvira Street. I guess I am getting used to everything here.

Well almost everything. I start Camp Big Sky today, for four weeks. It's the Jewish Center's summer camp. Oh boy. A big bus picks me up at

8:45 a.m. and I don't get home until 4 p.m... Again no one from the neighborhood or my class is going. But I am learning how to sing "I Come A Come A Zimba Ziya" and make lanyards. It's okay but I miss my friends. I wonder what they're doing but school will be starting soon. So that's good.

Daddy borrowed a special kind of camera, a movie camera, and big, very bright lights. He filmed me, Guy, Mommy and Kimmie walking inside our house. I started showing off so Mommy pushed me away onto my bed. It was hard to look at Daddy because the lights were so glary but I still can't wait to see the movie.

Mommy was cleaning the birdcage and Romeo flew away. He didn't come back.

I haven't seen Kanka in a long time and today Mommy and Daddy said he is in the hospital. Mommy says it's all in his head. I'm not sure what that means. And Mommy told Daddy that she doesn't want Aunt Ruth to *ever* set foot in our house. She said she is a *"vipère"*, a snake. Mommy is very angry with her. I think it's because Aunt Ruth is always fighting with Kanka and Daddy. And she always talks bad about everybody. Just like Great Aunt Pauline. Daddy says they are all lonely, scared people and they don't trust anyone, "miserable creatures", he calls them. He says he pities them. Oh dear. I hope I can visit Kanka soon.

Mommy is also going in the hospital to have an operation. She has to stay in the hospital for a while. She doesn't feel good a lot of the time. I hope this operation fixes her body. I don't think it's all in her head. Mrs. Sternberg, Harold's mommy, will take care of Guy and me during the day.

Today Daddy came home from the hospital and he looks tired but he wants to take me to the park. I am getting a fizzy feeling in my stomach. We don't usually go to the park like this. It's too late in the day. We get into the car but Daddy doesn't talk. We drive to La Cienega Park. He stops the engine, but Daddy doesn't move. He takes off his glasses. There are tears in his eyes. He tells me that Kanka is dead. I feel so sad because I didn't get to say goodbye. But I feel worse because my daddy is sad. I don't know what to do.

I don't go to the funeral. I've never been to a funeral but it's when you die and they put you in a box and bury you in the ground like buried treasure. No one asked me or told me to go. I'm not even sure when it was or where it was. Guy and I stayed with Harold next door.

Today was the first day of school. Daddy took me because Mommy is still in the hospital. I'm now in the fourth grade, B4, in Mrs. Zurmeullen's class. It's also in a bungalow. I wonder if I am ever going to have a class in the real building. Most of my friends from third grade are in my room again. There are some new friends, Terry and Margery.

Mommy is finally home from the hospital. It's been almost two weeks. Mrs. Sternberg was really nice to Guy and me but I'm glad Mommy is back. I didn't much like how Harold's mom cooked. Mr. Sternberg is kind of grumpy and the whole house smells like a wet dog. Mommy looks skinnier and she walks slow. And Kimmie is so happy to her, he jumps and jumps. Mommy doesn't like that. She says it hurts her body.

Today Mommy talked to the gardener and asked him if he would like to have Kimmie. He said yes. I don't understand why Kimmie has to leave. The gardener takes Kimmie home but Kimmie runs away and finds our house. Mommy has to call a taxicab and she takes Kimmie to the dog pound. I am so sad. Why is everything changing?

Today there is a spelling bee. I thought maybe we would have real bees but that's not the same thing. Anyway my word to spell is "sugar". I get it wrong; I spell it s-u-g-e-r. I feel stupid.

On Fridays after school I am now going to Al Gilbert's Dance Academy, not ballet, but tap dancing. I like the shiny black shoes and the leotard. A lot of the girls from my class are going, too. We are going to have a recital in December. (A recital is when you do a show and get to show off.)

Mommy has to go to the doctor almost every day to have radiation (?) treatments. Sometimes I go with her. I stay in the waiting room and thumb through the Highlights magazine, trying not to think. Mommy should be better now, it's been almost two months since she left the hospital. And she feels terrible afterwards, has a sore tummy and lots of diarrhea. She doesn't want to eat. She even smells different, kind of like the incinerator does after Daddy burns stuff. Shouldn't the treatments make her feel better, not worse? And she has to go back every day for more than a month!

Finally it's Mommy's last treatment, number 37!

Thanksgiving is sort of sad: Mommy, Daddy, Guy and I are not very happy. I think Daddy is missing his daddy. We didn't have turkey either. Mommy still doesn't feel too good and she's worried about her sister Mayie. Her family lives in Algeria and there's a lot of fighting over there. Every day Mommy waits for her letters but they don't come very often. But she said we are going to go to Palm Springs for Christmas vacation. I hope she feels better soon.

We went to visit Kanka's grave today. The place looks like a park but the trees are very small. I didn't see any people, just us. We put flowers where they buried Kanka. He's buried next to his sister Clara. Mommy prayed. Daddy didn't say anything. I feel a little scared.

Tonight is my first tap dancing recital. It's also an audition. I'm not sure what an audition is but Mommy draws a "beauty mark" on my face above my lip on the left side and puts red lipstick on me! The recital is fun but I didn't get picked for the audition. I tapped when I wasn't supposed to and I almost tipped over. Some girls that I don't know were picked. It's for a new television show called "The Mickey Mouse Club." I got lipstick and brown streaks on my pillow case during the night.

We are going to Palm Springs for Christmas but Mommy and Daddy gave us our presents early, before we left. I got a pair of roller skates (with a key), slippers and a basketball and basketball hoop. Guy got a cowboy outfit and some other stuff.

When we arrived at the first hotel Mommy didn't like it because it wasn't clean. So we moved to a brand new, just opened hotel. There's a swimming pool and a nice girl with short blonde hair is staying with her mommy and daddy next door. We swam together and went horseback riding too. Our family is staying a whole week. We visited the Salton Sea. We were going to fish but we didn't. Mommy found a dead little fish on the rocky, crusty beach. Tonight we went to a drive-in theatre. You stay in your car and watch the movie through the windshield and hang a box on your window glass so you can listen to the talking and music. I fell asleep.

Chapter 13:
Rotten Bananas 1957

Back at school, and it's been raining.

One of my classmate's daddy works for a television show, "I've Got a Secret," and today she passed out "I've Got a Secret" charm bracelets to some of us. I got one. She also gave out plastic owl key rings that glow in the dark. When I got home I showed Daddy the keychain and he took it and threw it away. He said it was dangerous, "It's 'radioactive'." And next day the teacher told everyone that got a bracelet they had to return it to our classmate because not every girl got one. I am disappointed and confused.

I am in trouble again. Being insolent. Mommy slapped me and told me to go my room. And she doesn't feel good again: back pains, stomach and headaches and it hurts when she goes *pipi*. She takes lots of pills. She typed a list of my chores and gave it to me.

Most days when I'm not in school I play with Harold next door or walk over to Harriet's house two blocks away.

I got a good report card: six A's. And I start in A4 and also Saturday French classes. Well, Mommy doesn't like the French school. She says it's dirty and disorganized. I only go one time.

I'm late to school today because Mommy feels terrible and has to stay in bed but I get to eat for the first time in the cafeteria. It's steamy waiting in the line for your food. But it smells real good. They served corn and hot dogs. And I also got to pick out a flying saucer cookie made by Mrs. Hardin the cook. It's huge!

I woke up in the middle of the night because Daddy banged his head on the bathroom door and fell down hard on their bedroom floor. I heard him groaning. Mommy had to open the little round bottle that's full of tiny, light yellow balls and put it under Daddy's nose. When he smelled it he woke right up, but he didn't look very good. It was kind of funny, but I feel worried.

Mommy got mad at me again today. She says I'm very selfish because I don't share anything with Guy. He breaks everything he plays with. But finally Guy has his own room. He got a new bed that he keeps falling out of.

On Sunday Daddy goes door-to-door collecting for the Heart Fund. Afterwards we all go to Granada Hills in the valley to see a house that Freddy (my dad's army buddy) wants to buy. We took the Sepulveda pass through the mountains then drove through lots of lemon and orange groves. The trees all blur together and the rows seem to turn like the spoked wheels of my bicycle. Big dry tumbleweeds rest near the side of the road. After, we eat at a restaurant called Love's Bar B-Q. You could smell it before we park the car. It's good. But on the way home the smudge pots' smoky smell is stronger than Love's.

Mommy still doesn't feel good. I think she goes to the doctor a lot. And she is trying to find someone to stay with Guy and me in May because Daddy and Mommy want to go back to France, I think. I also think that Mommy is worried because sometimes she doesn't pay attention to what I tell her. It's like she's listening to something inside her head.

I started a club at my house. Sue, Harold, Harriet, Richard, Carole and I are the members. We meet on Fridays in the playhouse in the backyard. I glued tiny envelopes in all the books I got from that older girl who used to live here. The members can check them out. Today we are cutting up old bed sheets that Mommy gave me to make autograph aprons. My friends say I'm bossy.

This weekend our family went driving to Pacific Palisades and Baldwin Hills looking at new houses. Mommy and Daddy seem real happy about the ones in Baldwin Hills. I hope they don't want to move again.

April: I went on a field trip to the Shrine Auditorium to see an opera, "Cinderella." It was okay but I really liked looking at the huge chandelier that was twinkling over my head, catching the light and spinning it into all the colors.

Mommy seems to be hurting all the time, being mad at me and feeling sad. And she's always taking pills, and waiting for letters from Lou Lou and her sister Mayie. Sometimes it's hard for her to walk so she lays down a lot. She stays in her pajamas and bathrobe all day.

I told Harriet that I heard Mommy and Daddy talking and that the doctor took two quarts of liquid out of Mommy's stomach. Harriet's daddy is a doctor.

Today was Mommy and Daddy's 11th wedding anniversary and we went to the Carthay Circle Theatre to see "Around the World in 80 Days." It was good and very long. There was an intermission and Mommy and Daddy bought me a souvenir book. The theatre is right behind the school yard. Guy stayed with Bert and Sally. Tomorrow is Easter.

I went to church with Mommy today. She seemed really sad. She lit a candle to St. Thérèse. We both prayed.

I went back to school and we had another field trip, this time to the San Gabriel mission. I wasn't really paying attention but I know there weren't any birds.

Some of Mommy and Daddy's friends took me to the circus. I don't know why their friends are taking me out so much.

I heard Mommy crying during the night. I couldn't go back to sleep, Mommy kept whimpering. Please make it stop. I can't stand it.

May: Today Daddy took Mommy to a place called City of Hope. I guess Mommy and Daddy are not going on vacation. They came home late. I'm getting bad headaches and I threw up today.

There was Open House at school again. Daddy went but Mommy had to stay home. My teacher said she might come and visit Mommy at home.

Today is Mommy's birthday but she had to go back to the City of Hope. Daddy said it's a kind of hospital. I don't understand what's going on. They came home very late. I hear her crying every night. Tonight she was vomiting and screaming. I try to hide, bury myself under the covers next to Mitou.

On Thursday Mrs. Zurmuellen, my teacher, came to visit Mommy.

Mommy lays on her recliner all the time now and Sally, Bert's wife, comes over a lot to cook for us. On Saturday she's going to take me to get a haircut.

May 15: Mommy is going to stay at the City of Hope for two weeks. Guy and I are staying with Sally and Bert tonight. On Saturday Guy and me stay next door at Harold's. Daddy drives to City of Hope every day to be with Mommy. Sometimes he comes home after dark.

On Sunday I am going with Daddy's friends Ruth and Hank to see a movie called "The King and I." Guy is going with some other friends of Daddy.

We got to visit Mommy today. The City of Hope is so far away from our house. Guy fell asleep and I just looked out the car window until we got there, fastening myself to the glass, watching it cloud up, putting my finger down, doodling. Watching my marks disappear.

Mommy was sitting in a chair outside. It's a little bit like a park with "cottages" that look like bungalows. She is staying in one of them. Children can't go inside. She looks tired but she was happy to see us.

May 27: Today we got a housekeeper. Her name is Arline and she will stay at our house, until Daddy gets home. I think I like her. I guess Daddy doesn't want to keep asking Mrs. Sternberg to watch us all the time.

May 31: Today is my 10th birthday and Daddy picked me up early from school, before lunch. Guy, me and Daddy go with Daddy's friends in their big, new car to see Mommy. I have a terrible headache and it's very hot. Daddy's friend's car has air conditioning and electric windows. You push a button and they go up and down. I don't feel good on the way to City of Hope. We stop to get me something for my tummy but I get sick while we are driving and I try to throw up out the window. Some of my throw up went inside the car door. Daddy's friend is mad. But I feel better, my headache went away. When we arrive we meet Mommy on the grass outside of her cottage, number 5. She's sitting in a wheelchair. There is a cake with a doll standing in the middle. The cake is supposed to be her skirt. I feel shy with Mommy.

I know it's only been two weeks since she's been away but I feel like I'm getting used to the house without her there, and that scares me.

Today at school I found out that I am being "skipped". That means that when I go back to school in September I will go to A5, not B5. Sue, Harriet and Taffy are also going to skip.

City of Hope, May 31, 1957

I also can bring home a real little frog if Daddy signs a paper.

I wrote Mommy a letter to send with Daddy. I told her about my frog and explained a word game that we can play together by mail.

Today at school Cindy's mother came into class and started yelling at my teacher. She's mad that Cindy didn't get skipped and said that the only reason I got skipped is because my mom's sick.

I was embarrassed and sad. I would go back into the second grade if would make Mommy get better faster. I just want to be a regular kid, just like everybody else.

Mommy's been gone almost four weeks. I don't miss her when I am at school but when I come home, I do. The housekeeper is nice I guess, but she's quiet, she doesn't really talk to me. Guy's still little so I can't really talk about Mommy with him. But I have the little paper Mommy typed of my chores. I try to do them. Mommy wrote me a letter back. Actually she sent back my letter and played the word game I put at the bottom of the page. She reminded me to drink enough water and take care of Guy and to make sure I leave water for the frog too. And that she loves me.

June 10: Mommy came home tonight. I was so excited to see her but she still doesn't feel well. She stays in her bathrobe and lays in bed all day. She's not very hungry either.

June 14: Mommy went back. Daddy says there's a new medicine the doctors want to give her.

June 21: Last day of school. Tomorrow we stay with Sally.

June 23: We visited Mommy today. We can only see her outside because children aren't allowed in her room. She looks very tired and her legs are all swollen. She still has to sit in a wheelchair because she can't stand up or walk but she was happy to see us. I hugged her and she squeezed me back. Her arms look okay.

I met one of her nurses. She's nice. She gave me a belated birthday present: a small statue of Jesus' Mommy, Mary, holding baby Jesus. (Daddy didn't seem to care that I got it.) I think there are doctors too but I haven't seen any. Afterwards Daddy took us to Van De Kamp's restaurant for dinner. Guy was very cranky. I was trying to make Guy quiet. He was embarrassing me. He kept hollering that he didn't want his food and that he needed a doctor! Daddy didn't say or do anything. We had to leave before we finished. Mommy would have been able to do something.

June 28: Mommy came home today and Daddy rented a special bed for her to sleep in. They delivered it before she came home. Mommy was crying in her room during the night. I covered my head with my pillow. I keep praying to God to make it stop and for Mommy to get better.

June 29: Daddy is giving Mommy shots. There's a thin, flat, black box that rests on top of their dresser that holds the thing he uses to give her each shot. It's called a syringe. It's very big and silver and glass. Lots of people are coming over to our house to visit Mommy. And the telephone rings all the time.

Mommy stays in bed, doesn't eat much and gets shots. Guy and I went to the beach today with Sally and Bert. It's been really hot and I am getting lots of headaches.

I go over a lot to the Sternberg's next door, Harold's house. I watch television with Harold and one of his older brothers in their den. Mostly

I watch Harold bite his toenails or I stare at this big painting called "Custer's Last Fight." It's horrible.

Today Daddy had a man put in a cooling machine in the window of their bedroom near Mommy's hospital bed.

Mommy was begging, screaming and crying last night. Please God make it stop.

July 24: Mommy went back to the City of Hope. I painted a picture of Mommy with my oil paints and gave it to Daddy to give to her. I think it really looks like her.

July 25: Sue came over with her bike and we rode up and down the driveway all day. I put my record player on the back porch with the electric cord pulled through the milk bottle chute. We listened to Pat Boone sing "Love Letters in the Sand" over and over while we rode in tight circles. Harold said we were crazy.

August 11: Daddy came home today early from visiting Mommy. He came inside and asked me to go for a ride to the park. I had that fizzy feeling in my stomach and when I opened the door to Daddy's car to get in, I saw the picture that I painted of Mommy laying on the front seat. Nobody told me that Mommy is dying but I know. I know what Daddy is going to tell me. We drive to the park in silence and I am thinking how it was just like when my Kanka died. Same ride, same park. My heart started to beat so hard. The sound filled my ears. Daddy turned to me and I think I said, "Mommy died". He started to cry and I didn't feel anything but I thought I should cry. So I did.

I slept with Daddy tonight.

August 13: Daddy asked me if I wanted to go to the funeral. I said "No". He shouldn't have asked me, he should have taken me. I was scared to go and didn't go. (Years later, a distant cousin who attended my mother's funeral told me it was a closed casket covered with white roses.)

Thump, thump, thump – I bounce the basketball over and over and over again. Sometimes I throw the ball towards the hoop. Thump, thump, all afternoon. Guy sits on the patio bench, sucking his thumb, with his blankie and watches me.

First day back at school. At recess, Harriet walked up to me and told me she knew that my mommy died and how sorry she felt. Again I felt that I was supposed to cry and so I did. I really didn't feel anything – not sad, not scared, not happy. Just nothing, like when you lay on your arm wrong and wake up and there's nothing. Before the pins and needles start.

My A5 class is in the main building, in room 19 on the second floor, and I have a man teacher, Mr. Gallagher. Most of my friends are in the same room. Our places are different than the big tables we sat at in the bungalows. Everybody sits at their own desk in rows, and the desks are nailed to the floor. There is a hole in the upper right side at the top of the desk. It's stained black and it has a faint smell. Somebody said they are inkwells but we don't use them.

Daddy took me to visit Mrs. Arkatov. She's a piano teacher and friend of Daddy's. She has two huge black pianos in her living room. They fit together like giant puzzle pieces. She showed me the pattern the black keys make on the tooth-colored ones: two black, three black, two black, three black over and over.

Daddy got me a used baby grand piano with Mrs. Arkatov's help. One of her students is going to give me lessons once a week. The piano is in our living room near the front window. Above the black and white keys are gold letters that spell "B-a-u-s". I think Mommy told Daddy that I should take lessons but I'm not sure. Sue is taking lessons too.

Dad got a new housekeeper after Arline left. This one's name is Anna. She has an accent that sounds like Sally and Bert. I think she's German. She sleeps at our house during the week, so Guy has to move back into my room. That's okay. Daddy had to buy another bed for Anna.

I got a small dark green book with a tiny lock on it. It's called a diary and it comes with a small gold key. You are supposed to write down what you did each day. I'll try to remember but there's not a lot of space to write my words.

October 5: Russian satellite named "Sputnik" was shot up.

Sunday, October 13: Daddy took us to visit Mommy's friends Louise and Iral and their kids in the valley. (They all speak French and English.) On the way home I was singing, "Eeny, Meeny, Miny, Moe, Catch a Nigger by the Toe." Daddy almost crashed the car he was so mad and told me never to say that again. I wasn't even sure what I said.

One of Louise's kids was singing it that way. I usually say "tiger". I thought Daddy was going to slap me on my face.

October 26: Anna left. I'm not sure why, but she left me her photograph. I think she liked Daddy too much. Anyway, today we got another new housekeeper. Her name is Janette. She'll sleep at our house during the week too. I had my first piano lesson in the morning. My teacher's name is Frances Itow. She's very nice and kind of quiet. I think she's Japanese. I went to the school Fiesta afterwards.

October 28: My first day practicing on the piano. I keep missing the right notes, keys. My fingers get tired too. This is harder than I thought.

October 29: I found my frog in the backyard. His body is two inches long and he has three inches of legs! I remember when he was just a tadpole. I'm making my costume for Halloween. I am going to be an Arabian.

November 2: Had my second piano lesson and wrote my cousin Caty in France. (I would find out many years later, from my godmother, that Guy and I were to move to France to be raised by Lou Lou and Louisette, Caty's parents, but my dad couldn't send us. Louisette felt that he would have probably completely fallen apart emotionally if we would have moved away.)

November 5: Today I got a letter from Walt Disney. The stationery is pretty – it has all the cartoon characters on it. I didn't really read it. I think it had something to do with Mommy's French friends or maybe Great Uncle Philip's store on Main Street at Disneyland. I don't know and I don't care.

November 6: I had a big fight with Daddy. He said I'm not helping, I forget to feed Mitou, I don't eat my food, I make faces and I talk back. Well, today I talked back again, loudly. Daddy is never home and all he does is stay in his room when he is home. And Guy is sick a lot. He gets lots of sore throats and he throws up too. And my lunch box smells like rotten bananas.

On the weekends Daddy mostly takes us to the movies, usually Westerns. Sometimes we go to Griffith Park. We go on the merry-go-round, the miniature train, or walk through Fern Dell. We don't talk much.

November 9: I had my third piano lesson. Francis says, "You're improving" because I can finally tuck my thumb under my third finger. Daddy took us to Farmer's Market for dinner. As usual, Guy kept hollering for the doctor while we were eating, screaming he's dying. He didn't eat at all and we had to leave before we were done.

November 17: Daddy took me and Guy and Harold to the snow at Mount Wilson. Then we went to the movies, "The 3:10 to Yuma". I ate some popcorn then fell asleep in my seat.

November 22: Daddy picked me up early from school today, and we went to Paramount Studios. Daddy's friend Mr. Panama took us on a tour. He's a director. I shook hands with Jerry Lewis and talked with Anthony Quinn. (I don't know who Anthony is.) But I stared at Yul Brynner while he practiced his words. Mr. Panama gave me two casting directories from 1955 and 1956. They look like the Yellow Pages but full of little pictures of people who pretend to be other people. We ate in the commissary. It's like a cafeteria except some people wear costumes.

November 28: Today is Thanksgiving Day. We went to the movies on Hollywood Boulevard.

November 29: We went to Uncle Philip's. Sometimes we eat there on Friday nights. We have lamb chops with mint jelly, a slice of cantaloupe with salt sprinkled on top, string beans and mashed potatoes. Uncle Philip sits at the head of the table, his brothers Morris and Charlie and his sister Pauline to his right and then us, on the left side. The food is served by a butler. Nobody talks. All these old people living together, eating the same thing every Friday night, it is strange and boring.

November 30: Today was my sixth piano lesson. Afterwards I went shopping with Sue to the May Company department store on the corner of Wilshire Boulevard and Fairfax Avenue. We walked. It only took about 20 minutes. I bought Christmas presents for Daddy and Guy. A Ticklebee game for Guy, and for Daddy, a tie with his initials, D.A. It cost almost four dollars! When we got home Sue showed me how to play "Chopsticks" on the piano and "Heart and Soul". She's a good teacher and she's only been taking lessons a few weeks longer than me.

December 3: Today we found out that Guy has to have his tonsils taken out.

December 4: Today the United States had planned to shoot up a Sputnik but it blew up. It was a flopnik.

December 9: Daddy took us to buy a Christmas tree.

December 12: Today Guy got a record to prepare him for his surgery. It's called "Peter Ponsil Lost his Tonsil."

December 13: Today was the last day of school before Christmas vacation. Harriet, Richard, Sue, Hyman and I did the play "The Night before Christmas." Funny, they're all Jewish.

December 14: Today Guy got his tonsils out and I went to Daddy's friend Sylvia's house for two days. She is teaching me how to knit. I like her house. It's very new. When you look out of the kitchen window across the street, sometimes you can see a cowboy riding on a horse. On one side of the street there's a sidewalk and a row of new houses but on the other side, for as far as you can see, there's nothing but dirt and cows.

December 17: Guy's home and he has to stay in bed all day. He gets to have ice cream and Jell-O, but he won't eat anything.

December 20: Guy is feeling better. We play basketball in the backyard with Harold, and have lunch outside.

December 25: Daddy got me a set of California rocks and minerals. They're glued on to a piece of cardboard. There are 36 different rocks and minerals, each with their name printed under them. I like the asbestos one best because I can peel it.

December 31: I tiptoed into Daddy's room. He fell asleep on Mommy's recliner in front of the TV. The Indian head test pattern was watching him. I turned off the TV and went back to bed.

Chapter 14:
Buried Treasure 1958

I started the New Year sick and I was absent from school for the first week. I had a cold and a headache. I watched some of the Rose Parade on television with Daddy and Guy. (We used to be able to see part of the parade from our backyard in Pasadena).

When Daddy is home from work he doesn't talk much. He mostly stays at his desk cutting out articles from magazines and newspapers. Sometimes he goes out at night and plays chess. I think he's missing Mommy. If I start thinking about Mommy, I make myself start thinking about something else.

But on weekends Daddy usually takes us to the movies, the beach or the park. We go out to dinner at Van de Kamp's a lot. Sally, Silvia or Mrs. Sternberg, Harold's mom, sometimes takes care of us too. Like today, I went with Harold and his family to a potluck picnic at a park. They have so many friends and relatives. Everyone brought something to share. It was nice.

I was invited to Lanny's party. He's a cute short boy in my class. We played "kissing games" and I kissed almost every boy! On Saturday mornings I mostly go with Harold to the Picfair Theatre to see the matinee. It's full of kids and real noisy. We watch serials. There was a real good one about a boy with super powers who could hit a baseball real fast and far. The kids in the audience throw the tops of their ice cream cups at the screen and sometimes the lids stick. I don't.

February: I start the B6 today with Mrs. Chaldu and I am back in a bungalow. Guy turned five years old today and it is his first day in kindergarten. He's in the main building, in Mrs. Becker's room 14. They have their own playground so I don't see him.

A new girl from another school started today and she sits next to me. Her name is Diane.

Daddy is 46 years old today and I love him very, very, very, very, very, very much.

The school nurse passed out Permission Slips to most of the sixth grade girls. I didn't get one. If your mom signs the slip, you have to see a special health movie. Me and another girl play on the yard instead.

March 13, Thursday: Today we celebrated Arbor Day at school and I got picked to help dig a hole and plant a small pine tree on the side of the school near the sidewalk. The teacher took pictures for the New Pioneer, the school magazine. Some of the girls said I only got picked because my mom died.

March 22, Saturday: I went with Harold and his mom downtown. We took the bus because she doesn't drive. We had lunch at a place called Clifton's Cafeteria. It was decorated like a jungle and you could pick out your own food just like at the school cafeteria. While we were waiting for the bus home, the newspaper boy was calling out that there had been a plane crash, somebody named Mike Todd was killed. He was married to a movie star.

March 28, Friday: Today was Harriet's last day at Carthay. She's moving away to "the Valley" next week. We gave her a going away party and I gave her a Nancy Drew book.

On Saturday Harriet, Guy and I went to see "Snow White and the Seven Dwarfs" and "Tammy and the Bachelor." I am going to miss her. But we have promised to be pen pals. I remember a long time ago that I went to see "Snow White" with Mommy. And that it scared me. It didn't scare me this time but missing someone does.

April: Today while Daddy and Guy went to the beach, I went to Aunt Pauline's apartment to swim. I had a terrible time. She asked me why I didn't like Aunt "Root", Daddy's sister Ruth. I didn't answer. Pauline's lips looks like a clown mouth. She doesn't color inside the "lines."

Tonight I think Daddy went out to play chess and he said he would be back in time to put Guy to bed. He was late and Jeanette, our housekeeper, smacked Guy over and over for not going to bed. I hate her. I'm telling on her.

School is terrible lately. Diane had to move seats because the boys were talking. Barry hates me and I hate Terry, Sue and Cindy.

May 4, Saturday: Sally took me and Guy out shopping. I got new shoes, socks and a bathing suit and a good lunch and dinner.

May 5, Sunday: Daddy took Harold, Guy and me to the beach. Guy wandered away and we couldn't find him. Finally we did. We ate dinner at one of Daddy's friend's apartment. It looks over the ocean. It was a nice day except for Guy getting lost for a while.

May 6, Monday: I got terrible grades today, a 70% on my spelling test and 80% on my division problems. After dinner Daddy and Guy walked to the 5 & 10 & 25 Cent store. I walked with my across-the-street friend Susan M. We got separated and Daddy got mad at me. I think he was worried but I explained.

May 8, Wednesday: I got 100 percent on two tests and got to interview a teacher, Mrs. Frakes, because she's retiring. (That means she's finished being a teacher.) Tonight, Silvia and Jon and their daughter Simone came over to show us their new tape recorder. You can hear music and singing just like a record and record player but it uses brown cellophane tape and it's called "stereo." When they put on the demonstration tape it sounded like a real bowling ball was rolling across our living room floor. And best of all you can also record your own voice or any sound and play it back. I stayed up until 10:30.

Today would have been Mommy's birthday. She would have been 37 years old.

May 9, Friday: Today Daddy found out he can't drive his car on our street because they are going to dig it up to put in a new storm drain. I slept with Daddy tonight.

May 10, Saturday: Today I went to Pickwick Stables. I'm taking horseback riding lessons.

May 13, Tuesday: I have to write a report about the St. Lawrence Seaway. I am having a hard time getting started so Daddy is helping me but he's really just writing it for me. I copied what he wrote. I know it's not okay but I did it anyway. Daddy knows and he doesn't care. I don't like it that I can't think of the words to write all by myself.

May 14, Wednesday: Daddy found my frog. He's as big as two of Daddy's fists! And the diggers found some huge bones in front of our house too. They had to stop digging and wait for the men from the museum to come and examine the bones.

May 15, Thursday: The bones are fossils from a giant Imperial Wooly Mammoth! All the digging has to stop so that the people from the museum can carefully take them out. This is really exciting! They are right in front of our house. The story is in the newspaper on the front page. I wrote Harriet to tell her all about it.

May 17, Saturday: I went to a party this afternoon and danced with a lot of boys and I kissed Barry twice!

May 19, Monday: I wore my new sack dress to school and Sue and I are making flying machines that you wear on your wrist like a watch. The museum people came to school with some of the fossils.

May 22, Thursday: I passed out my birthday invitations. Everyone can come. Sue and I made ring flying machines and they made a hit with Barry. I'm doing very well with Barry.

May 23, Friday: Today I got my first piece of sheet music, "The Tarantella."

May 24, Saturday: We got a new housekeeper, her name is Flora. Jeanette was terrible. Sally took me to Uncle Bernie's Toy Menagerie to get party favors.

May 27, Tuesday: Got in a real big fight with Daddy. I was trying to explain to him about my birthday party. I don't want him in the room with us all the time, Sally is going to help. He won't listen to me.

May 31, Saturday: Everyone came to my house for my party. I am now 11. It was okay. Daddy borrowed a film projector and showed old cartoons and a Laurel and Hardy movie in the living room. I felt a little embarrassed of Daddy being there and I kept thinking that my friends really didn't want to be at my party. Sally helped serve cake and ice cream. I got good presents though: days-of-the-week underpants, a paint-by-the-numbers kit and handkerchiefs. Barry gave me a bottle of perfume.

June 2, Monday: Daddy got me a white tape recorder (a Wallensak) just like the one Sylvia and Jon brought over. I really like it. Before Daddy returned the film projector we watched the movie that he made of Mommy, me and Guy last year. It didn't last very long.

June 9, Monday: My teacher is not fair and the girls in my room make me sick. I had another fight with Sue about practically nothing. We made up later.

June 18, Wednesday: I went to a piano recital and saw my teacher and a girl from school. I didn't play. I went to bed really late.

June 20, Friday: Today is the last day of school. I got a good report card: 10 A's, 1 B and 1 B+ and all Outstandings. Then I got my hair cut all off. It's real short: a pixie cut. I think Mommy would have liked it. And I found a black kitten in the back yard. Daddy said we can keep it.

June 23, Monday: Diane and I made lemonade and we sold it to all the men digging in front of our house. We made lots of money: we charged 5 cents a cup and made $2.45! But Guy went into the hole and the men had to bring him out. I named the kitten "Kitty".

June 27, Friday: We sold lemonade again until it was time for me to leave for Harriet's new house. I'm staying there overnight. It's a beautiful brand new house!

June 30, Monday: Sold lemonade with Diane again.

July 1, Tuesday: Alaska was made the 49th state. (Harriet's grandparents went to Alaska and brought her back some souvenirs. She gave me the miniature sealskin shoes that they got her.) Guy cut his lip and we went to the doctor's. He's okay.

July 4, Friday: Daddy took us to see the fireworks at the Coliseum. It was awful except for the part when they turned off all the lights and everybody lit a match.

July 13, Sunday: We got rid of the old housekeeper and got a new lady named Kit Slaughter. (I don't like her last name.) She stays only till Daddy comes home from work so I get my room back!

Sue came back from her vacation. She took the train to Las Vegas. She said she went to a strip tease show with her parents. She said lots of ladies were dancing with hardly any clothes on! She said she wasn't supposed to see it. Wow.

We will be going on vacation too. We're going to the Highland Inn. It's near the mountains. Daddy said I can invite Harriet.

Our new housekeeper Kit always listens to the radio. I asked her why all the songs are about love. All she said is that I need to be careful with boys and that I have nice feet. I think she wants to marry Daddy. She's not his type.

July 20: Daddy took us to Fern Dell in Griffith Park. I caught five guppies that were swimming in the creek. I used an empty jar. Guy couldn't catch any. Daddy said I could bring them home. I put the jar with the guppies on the counter in the breakfast room. I fed them some turtle food. They liked it.

July 21: When I went into the breakfast room this morning I found all the guppies stabbed with toothpicks on a towel lying on the counter! Guy did it. I was so sad and mad. Daddy yelled at Guy. Guy is crazy.

July 27: Sally took me to the Lerner's Shop to buy a bra. All the girls in my class wear them and the boys pull the back and snap them. The bra is a size 28 AAA, a training (?) bra. The saleslady said I didn't really need it but Sally bought it for me anyway.

July 28: Today I put Elmer's Glue on my nipples and sprinkled blue glitter on them and danced in front of the big mirror in the bathroom. Daddy walked in and he looked like he was going to faint.

He tried to give me a "talk" later about babies and stuff. I told him I already knew. He looked happy and walked out of my bedroom.

July 29: I got home from playing at Sue's and found Guy in my room. I yelled at him to get out. When I looked around I noticed that he moved my special box of 16 decorated Jordan Almonds that Mommy gave me. (Each one was decorated in a tiny costume to look like people from around the world.) I was saving them. I wasn't ever going to eat them. He licked every one so they were all plain white. I hate him!!

July 30: When I got home today my Smith-Corona typewriter was in a million pieces!!! Guy is terrible. Daddy is real mad at him.

August 1: Guy fixed my typewriter! <u>All by himself</u>. I can't believe it. He's only five and half years old. It really works.

August 11: Today Daddy took Guy and me to Holy Cross Cemetery to visit Mommy's grave. We brought some daisies and Daddy took pictures. I don't know how I felt. Guy just ran around on the grass. On the way home we saw a dead horse lying on the street. A girl was standing next to it crying.

August 17: Today we leave for the Highland Inn with Harriet. Daddy is driving us: Guy, Harriet and me. We're staying for one week.

I should be having fun here but I don't feel like I want to have fun. I am mean to Harriet. I know I'm being mean to her but I can't stop myself. There are lots of activities but I am not interested. A record player is playing "The Tennessee Waltz" in the background, kids are laughing and dancing. I just can't make my inside feelings match the way my outside acts. I can't help myself and I don't ask for help. I know I'm being a brat but I don't know how to stop.

Daddy is painting a big portrait of Mommy with oil paints. His easel is set up in a corner of their bedroom. He asked me to "sit" for Mommy while he paints. I don't think I look like her much but he wants me to sit anyway. He paints when he gets home from work and now it's almost finished. It looks just like Mommy. He put it away in the closet.

Daddy is still cutting out articles and now he's putting them in a kind of scrapbook. I peeked at it when he wasn't home. All the newspaper and magazine pieces are about cancer. That's what Mommy had, cancer.

September: I am now in the A6. I'm back in the main building upstairs. My new teacher is also a man like last year. He's name is Mr. Lacoeur. That means "the heart" in French. He's very cute and all the girls are in love with him. Today he gave us our spelling list for the week. Our test will be on Friday. We all giggled when we read the list. Two of the words were: girdle and brazier. Diane thinks he might get in trouble with the principal.

October: Daddy is going out with some ladies. We usually go out all together to an amusement park or restaurant. One of them is a widow, her husband died. (Daddy is a widower.) I think she has kids but I'm not sure. After we came home Daddy asked me what I thought of her and if she would be a good mommy. I told him that that he has to live with her and I can't tell him what to do. Why does he ask me stuff like this? He's the grown-up, not me.

We went to Disneyland with a different lady. Freddy and his wife Lisa came too. I guess I wandered away. I wasn't lost but when Freddy found me, he shook me and yelled that I worried Daddy and I was terrible to do that to him. I didn't say anything.

Daddy brought home another lady. She has blonde hair and blue eyes. And her name is Judy. She's a friend of Sylvia and Jon. She's Hungarian like Sylvia. They belong to the same Hungarian club. Jon is French like Mommy was. He met my mommy at a French club meeting. Anyway Judy has a son named Andrew. He's older than me and they both have an accent. There's no husband or daddy. She's not a widow, though.

Daddy is seeing Judy a lot. I think Guy likes her. Do we need another mommy? I guess it's cheaper than having a housekeeper. But I already have a mommy, I can't replace her like my shoes.

I think I love Shelly. He's in the A6 too, but he's not a good student. He gets in trouble a lot. He has long shiny black hair that he wears in a DA (Duck Ass). He combs his hair back and makes a ridge to his collar (that he turns up) and then combs the rest of his hair in front so it curls and hangs over his forehead and keeps the comb in his back pocket. Sometimes he uses bad words but I like him. He's a "greaser," a bad boy, but I really like him.

After school I usually go to the gas station that's behind the school playground next to the Cathay Circle Theater. You can buy candy, baseball cards and wax lips there. It's a little scary because it's so dark where you go in. A creepy guy sells me Lik-M-Aid candy and some flag cards that come with a thin card-size pink sheet of bubble gum. (Flag cards are like baseball cards but each one has a picture of a flag from a different country.) Some days when we walk home we take the secret sidewalk, Santa Ynez Way. It goes right through the middle of the block that's across from school. It's a short cut. And on both sides of the walkway there are still some yellow honeysuckle blossoms left on the vines that cover the walls. You bite the thin end of the flower and suck out the drop of sweetness. I taste it only for a second but it's worth it. And then there are pomegranates! They hang over another backyard wall along the walk. We pick one and peel it and get pink stains all over but it's so good.

Friday, October 31: I'm invited to Sandy R.'s Halloween party. She lives on Crescent Heights, near where Harriet used to live. I'm dressed as a mummy. I made my own costume by wrapping toilet paper over and over my arms, my body and my legs but the best part is my face. I carefully cracked an egg and saved the two halves of the shell. Then I put a hole in the center of each half and painted red squiggly lines coming from the holes. Then I glued the edges and stuck them over my eyes. I can see straight ahead and when I look in the mirror I'm real scary. The party is fun but it was kind of spooky walking home alone. There was that warm wind and I could hardly see where I was going. I gave myself goose pimples. (Oh, I won a goldfish at the school fall festival.)

November: Daddy, Guy and me went to dinner at Sally and Bert's. They live in a cute little house on Cherokee Street in Hollywood. I got to play outside with Howard, their son. He's older, maybe three years. Anyway Howard took his baseball bat and ball and he was showing me how to swing the bat. He's tall and strong. When he took his turn he hit the ball so hard it flew over the house and then we heard a sound like breaking glass. Uh oh! I wanted to go back inside but Howard said we need to see what happened. We walked up to his neighbor's front door and knocked. The old lady that lives there opened the door and was very upset. She said that ball broke her glass washboard. Howard apologized and said he would get her a new one. (He's a Boy Scout.) Then we went back to Howard's house and he explained to his daddy and mommy what happened. Howard acts like a grown up. I hope I can be like him someday.

December: On Saturday Sue and I walk to Pico. We go up and down all the aisles at the 5 & 10 & 25 Cent Store and then we go through the connecting side door to Fox's Big Town Market for our lunch. Right around the corner inside is a little pizza pie stand with four stools to sit on. I buy a slice of mushroom pizza pie and a coke. It cost 30 cents. It's delicious. After we finish we walk over to the magazine rack. They sell paperback books, too. Sue shows me "Lady Chatterley's Lover" and "Peyton Place." There are dirty parts in them. The man from the market tells us to put the books down. He says we're not old enough to look at them. Sue decided we should walk over to the pickle barrel. You use the big tongs to fish them out. It costs a nickel but the pickle is huge and good. I guess we're old enough for pickles.

Sometimes I walk to the dime store alone. Today I decided to kiss each palm tree on our side of the street all the way up to Pico – three blocks. My lips are sore. I'm not sure why I did it. I think maybe it's because

I don't like the way they look and I'm sorry that I feel that way. Or that it will bring me good luck. I know. I'm really weird. But being at the dime store alone is like going to church for me. It's soothing to walk the aisles, sort of like Mommy used to do with her rosary.

I think that Uncle Philip is closing his factory. That means that Daddy is going to have to find a new job. I think Uncle Philip is retiring like Mrs. Frakes did.

Daddy gave me his tiny chess set he used while he was in the Army and he tried to teach me how to play. I learned all the special moves the different pieces make but I'm not really interested.

Judy and Andrew had Christmas with us but I think that they're Jewish. Also Andrew told me he lived with his grandmother until he was 12 years old, not his mom. (He's 15 ½ now.) They lived in Hungary and then he had to go live with his mother because of the Hungarian Revolution and the Communists. Judy lived in London, England then. Then he and his mother moved to White Plains, New York, then Los Angeles. His grandmother stayed in Hungary. Andrew goes to Fairfax High School. After the A6 I will be going to junior high school. In February.

Judy has big shoulders, long painted fingernails and wears high heels. She's taller than me but not as tall as Mommy. I think she's younger than Mommy would have been. She says that she's a very good swimmer and diver. And she said she also used to do ballet dancing.

Today Judy took me to Dr. Doolittle's Dance Store and got me black satin toe shoes! We also got pink furry things you put over your toes so they don't hurt when you go on your toes. It still hurts. She said she will teach me how to dance on my toes.

Chapter 15:
Check Mate 1959

January: Judy, Andrew, Freddy and Lisa came over for dinner on the first day of the year. I decorated the dining room.

Judy is real nice to me. She works at the I. Magnin store at the Charles of the Ritz Salon. It's at the very top of the store, the penthouse floor. I think Mommy went there sometimes. Judy gave me a new lipstick, "Miss Ritz." And she gave me nail polish ("Gold Gold") the next day. I think she wants me to like her.

My class is graduating soon. That means that we will be having many special activities. First we are going to Olvera Street downtown for an A6 fieldtrip, then we take a group picture in front of the school and then we lead the whole school assembly by the flagpole. The last thing is the dance.

February: Guy turned six! Daddy rented a van and painted the outside: "Guy's Birthday Bus". (The paint is washable.) We went to the Beverly Park and Ponyland with some of Guy's friends from school. Drew and Tiffany are his best friends. Beverly Park has a Ferris wheel, merry-go-round and lots of other rides, mostly for little kids. I went on the Haunted Castle ride all by myself but I didn't really like it. It was cool and dark inside, with a burnt smell and loud banging doors. I should have asked Daddy to ride with me. On the way home, the man on the radio said that a plane crashed and some rock and roll singers died: the Big Bopper, Buddy Holly and Ritchie Valens. I liked the Big Bopper.

Daddy enrolled me in the Ann White Drama Group. It's at a very proper lady's big house. Sue is going too, so that's good. We meet two times a week after school and we'll put on a performance at the end of June.

Today Judy took me shopping at I. Magnin to buy a dress for the A6 dance. I also had to get a hoop underskirt to hold the dress out. It's very fancy but kind of scratchy underneath. Then she took me to the Charles of the Ritz beauty salon to get my hair and nails done!

The dance was okay. I didn't get asked to dance much. All the girls were giggling, squealing. Not me though.

I took my Brownie to school for Camera Day today. We took turns taking each other's picture. I stood against the bungalow wall pretending I was being "shot" by Castro for one photo.

Judy took me shopping again, this time for some new clothes for junior high school. We went to Bullock's. I told her that's where Mommy would buy me clothes. I got a beautiful royal blue two piece wool outfit (a pleated skirt and matching middy top with white trim) and white buck saddle shoes. And a powdery buck pad to keep my shoes clean and white. I think Mommy would have liked my outfit.

February 16: Today I started John Burroughs Junior High School. I'm a B7, a "scrub." I love the buildings. It sort of reminds me of San Rafael Elementary School in Pasadena. Uncle Philip's mansion is two blocks away. Daddy drove me to school. And today is his birthday.

It's really different from elementary school. You have six different classes each day. And you have to take gym and wear special gym clothes. And you have a homeroom that's different from the other six classes, and a locker with a combination. My homeroom teacher is Mr. Harris, room 108. The bell is always ringing and there's a loudspeaker in every room for announcements. Some of my classes are upstairs but you have to remember to go up only on the "Up Staircase" and down the "Down Staircase" or you'll get a citation from the Space Patrol. (The Space Patrol is a bunch of older kids that wear sashes and stand at the top and bottom of the stairs to make sure you follow the rules.)

And there's a strict dress code. Girls have to wear a full slip and the hem of your skirt or dress has to be below your knees. Your shoes have to have laces and at least six eyelets each. There's even a rule for your socks: they can't be rolled down below your anklebone! And no make-up. Boys have to have their shirts tucked in and wear a belt or suspenders. If you don't follow the rules, you get punished. If you're a boy you get paddled by Mr. Hunt, the Boys' Vice-Principal. I don't know what they do to the girls.

There will be a Mother-Daughter Tea next week but I won't go. Also there are lots of papers to fill out with your name, address, telephone number, mother's and father's name. Mr. Harris told me how to spell "deceased."

I like my sewing class. We're learning how to use a real sewing machine. We're also learning how to embroider and make a knot on a thread with one hand. Your name has to be on your gym clothes, so we're copying our handwriting with black embroidery thread on the white stripe on the shorts and on the blouse pocket. We have to use a thimble. It's like a little metal hat that your right middle finger wears. We also have to make a 'ditty bag' (?) to hold our dirty gym clothes to take home on Fridays, and an apron and potholder for our cooking class. Our sewing teacher is named Mrs. Walker. She's tiny, with white hair that she wears in a bun. She's very old.

Our English teacher is Miss Ebbets. She's tall, thin and also old. She stands in front of the class and taps her cane on the floor. We will be learning poems that we will have to memorize and recite in front of the class. She scares me.

I also have my homeroom teacher, Mr. Harris, for a social studies class. I like him. He's tall and thin and the sides of his face are flat. He kind of looks like a tall fish. He has a booming voice but I still like him a lot.

My gym class is the most uncomfortable class for me. You have to change into your gym clothes and then take a shower after class. The dressing room is a little bit like the locker room at the Jewish Center. Every one changes in front of each other and there are no doors on the showers. I don't usually take showers at home, only a bath once a week and a face, feet and fanny wash every morning.

But a good thing, though. One time when I walked into the gym, I suddenly got a whiff of something I'd forgotten that made me remember when I was very little. It's the smell of the fancy cage elevator in Paris. I wish I could save it and put in a bottle like perfume or replay it over and over like one of my 45's. It reminded me of Mommy. I hope I smell it again.

I've met a lot of new kids. Not everyone from Carthay went to John Burroughs. Some went to Louis Pasteur. And not all the kids are Jewish. There are even some colored kids.

Most of the kids are a lot bigger than me, even the B7's. I really notice how small I am in gym class. I used to be one of the tallest girls, but maybe because I skipped a grade, I'm not anymore. And some girls have got their periods but not me.

Today I almost walked into the Boys Lavatory. When I found the Girls', there was a ninth grader (I think) slowly ratting her hair in front of the mirror. I could see her eyes staring at me while I washed my hands. She didn't smile and then she hid a real razor blade in between her ratted hair above her bangs. I froze. It might have been better if I had gone into the Boys Lavatory. And I'm sure she was wearing make-up.

I watch the older girls a lot: how they stand, leaning on one hip, holding their blue cloth 3-ring notebooks.

March: Today Mrs. Walker, my sewing teacher, was checking our basting. We were all lined up by the table where she sits. She always is sitting. Anyway, when she was looking at my stitching, she said my knot was as big as a clodhopper. I said, "Oh God". She looked up suddenly and said, "What did you say?" I was confused. I didn't know what I did wrong. I did not say one more word, I was just stunned and trying to think. Drurrie who was standing right behind me, jumped into the conversation and said to Mrs. Walker, "She said, 'Oh gosh'." For a moment, Mrs. Walker just stared at me. Then she told me to go back to my seat. It took me awhile to understand what had happened. I thanked Drurrie.

After the bell rings at 3:15 I usually walk home with Sue and Diane. We walk down McCadden Drive to Wilshire Boulevard then we walk past the La Brea Tar Pits. Sometimes we walk through the park and get tar on the bottoms of our shoes. We could take the bus, but it's more fun walking and talking. Sometimes we stop at Carnation's or Thrifty Cut-Rate Drug Store and Bar and Grill for French fries and a cherry coke. I usually get home by 4:30.

There's a funny song on the radio called "Tan Shoes and Pink Shoelaces". I told Daddy about it and told him he should make them. I said if he gave them to the popular kids, everyone would want them and make their parents buy them. He laughed. I hope he makes them.

One day I took the bus on Wilshire. Instead of going toward home, though, I went towards downtown and got off at the I. Magnin store. I met Judy upstairs. She's the receptionist and she re-introduced me to the ladies and men that fix people's hair and paint their nails. Then she took me to the Girls Department and bought me a charm bracelet. (It isn't real gold though.)

Daddy talked to me and Guy today and told us that he is going to marry Judy and she is going to be our new mommy. Guy seemed happy. I guess it's okay. It's really Daddy's decision, but he didn't ask me like last time though. He already decided. And she seems nice but she's not Mommy. Andrew will be moving to our house too. They're going to get married next month in Las Vegas.

Guy, Daddy and me went to visit where Judy and Andrew live. It's called a "courtyard" apartment. It's very small and there are two other apartments attached to theirs and another three right across the little courtyard. It's on busy Fairfax Avenue, way past the May Company department store, towards Hollywood Boulevard.

April: Andrew and Judy moved in and Daddy and Judy flew to Las Vegas. Guy had to move back into my room and Andrew got his old room. We don't have our housekeeper anymore because Judy quit her job.

In the middle of the night, Guy woke up because Kitty was having kittens right on top of him in his bed! He didn't know what was going on. Andrew had to come in and pull one baby that slipped between the wall and Guy's bed. It was funny. Kitty had six kittens! They're so cute.

Well, Daddy and Judy are home. Am I supposed to call her Mommy? Guy seems real comfortable with her but I notice that Andrew and Judy argue a lot. I'm not sure, though, because they're talking loudly in Hungarian, but Andrew walks away then slams the door to his room so I'm pretty sure.

Judy cooks real good dinners but when Andrew and Judy eat breakfast, it's really strange. They eat sandwiches. They spread chicken fat (it's in a jar they keep in the refrigerator) on toasted seedless rye bread, then slice onion and put that on top of the chicken fat. Then they eat it! And they drink lots of seltzer water that gets delivered like the milk, except the bottles are taller and have a pump. Daddy calls it 2 cent plain. (?) It makes me burp.

May: I came home today and the kittens were gone! Judy/Mom said that she sent them to the pound. Kitty is still here but she shouldn't have done that. She didn't even say anything about it first. And on the news, they said that the police pulled people out of their own homes near downtown and bulldozed them! They're going to build a baseball stadium on their property. That's not fair!!

My birthday was okay. I'm 12. We went to the Pickwick Pool in the Valley. It's a huge round pool with diving boards on a little island in the middle of the pool. Judy/Mom swam to the center doing the breaststroke. She never put her head in the water. Then she climbed out on the diving platform, did a handstand and climbed up the ladder balancing on her hands!! Then she walked on her hands to the end of the board and did a back dive into the water. My friends were impressed. I think she was showing off.

June 16: Andrew got a long distance phone call from his grandmother. He was so happy to talk to her. He said she said to say "hello" to me. She only speaks Hungarian. It was his birthday, he's 16, his Golden Birthday. Andrew wants to get a driver's license. And I think he wants to get a car, too.

School is almost over for the summer. I'm liking J.B. better. I'm getting used to the routine. Daddy has been driving carpool every day. Sue and Diane come too, but their fathers don't take a turn. But it's okay because I like being with Daddy in the car every day.

Our Drama Group had our performance today. All the girls wore hats and gloves and the boys wore suits. I didn't have a very big part but I told a joke about planting birdseed so you could grow baby birds. Everybody laughed. Daddy came.

I met a real cute, nice boy. He's the son of one of Daddy's business friends. Daddy, Judy/Mom, me and Roger and his parents, took a long drive out to a real nice restaurant called Padua Hills. (Guy and Andrew didn't go.) There were musicians, too. Roger and I went walking by ourselves after dinner behind the restaurant where there is an outdoor theatre. It was dark and empty, but warm and the wind was blowing a little. Roger kissed me. He has soft lips. The kiss gave me shivers. It wasn't like the kind of kisses that you get playing kissing games like Spin the Bottle or Post Office. Roger doesn't live near me or go to school at J.B. I hope Daddy stays friends with his dad.

Bert and Sally don't come by much anymore. I miss them.

July: I'm not going to camp and I don't think we're going on any vacations. I think Daddy is busy trying to start a new business. Tonight, I could see the search lights crisscrossing the sky from my window. I guess there's a premiere for a new movie at the Carthay Circle Theatre.

I talk on the telephone with Sue and Diane almost every day. Some days I walk with Sue to Pico but that's getting boring. Her older brother goes to the bowling alley next door to the record store so we're going to go too.

I'm not very good at bowling yet but it is funny watching the pin boys running at the end of the alley setting up the fallen pins. All you can see is their legs. We're also taking the bus down Pico Boulevard to Westwood Boulevard. There's another shopping place there. I think it used to be the small amusement park that we would go to with Mommy. I'm not sure though. I didn't pay enough attention. I am forgetting her. On the bus, I stare out the window, breathing close to the glass, watching it cloud up. I put my finger down, draw a face. I sit back and watch the face slowly disappear.

The shopping place has a J.J. Newberry's variety store. There's a downstairs like Woolworth's in Pasadena. And there's another bowling alley but we haven't tried it. Next door, I like the soft buns at the 19 cent hamburger place called Scot's and the candy and ice cream store McFarland's. I can get red shoelace licorice for a penny apiece. Sue always has more money to spend than I do, though. I think I'll ask Daddy if I can get an allowance.

In a few days I'll start summer school at Louis Pasteur. That's the other junior high school I could have gone to. It lasts four weeks. You can take one or two classes. I'm taking two: Algebra and Art. Nobody from J.B. is in either of my classes.

Well, I got sick. I got the German measles and missed three days of school so they dropped me! It's not fair but they won't let me come back. I didn't like it much anyway. But while lying in bed, I found an article in Life magazine about teenagers and allowances. I'm not a teenager yet but it gave me some ideas how to convince Daddy to give me an allowance.

August: Today Sue and I took the bus all the way to Hollywood Boulevard! We had to get a transfer, but it was fun. We walked from one end of the boulevard to the other and back. It has a lot of hamburger stands and little outlet stores that sell all kinds of stuff, mostly things made in Japan. The smell of grilled onions and grease followed us the whole way. We spent all day there.

On Sundays we, Daddy, Guy, Andrew, Judy/Mom and I usually go on drives. My stepmother (I don't say that to her face) likes to go places that have pools. She loves to swim. Andrew teases me and Guy in the back seat. Guy laughs. Andrew has a funny accent: he says V's for W's and W's for V's. (Judy/Mom has an accent too, but it's not funny-sounding, more like Zsa Zsa Gabor's.) Anyway I'm not sure what I think about Andrew. He's my stepbrother and I call him Andrew or Andy. It's easier than figuring out what to call my stepmother. I don't think Daddy likes Andrew very much but I'm not sure.

I'm thinking that my stepbrother likes me. Maybe too much. Sometimes when we're alone at home, he has me sit on his lap. I like him but he's supposed to be my brother. I'm so mixed up. And he's nice but he has a big nose and his accent sometimes bothers me. He has a lot of friends. Almost all of them are also Hungarian. They come over a lot.

Andrew seems to be arguing all the time with his mother and he doesn't talk much with my daddy but Daddy doesn't talk much with anyone. Daddy is so busy with his work. When he comes home he lies down on the recliner in their bedroom then he falls asleep under the newspaper. I see him at dinner but we're not allowed to talk at the table. It's funny, though. My girlfriends found out that we can't answer the telephone during dinner so they make sure that they call at dinnertime so that the telephone interrupts our "silence." It's so stupid. No one gets up to answer the telephone and it just keeps ringing and ringing.

September: Well, Andrew told me he loves me! ("*Szeretlek*" in Hungarian.) I'm not sure how I feel. School is starting again. I haven't said anything to Sue or Diane about Andrew but I think that they know. Anyway I have a lot of homework. And I still see Roger from time to time but he wears braces now. Andrew is always laughing at me. Harry (Harold), from next door, is now hanging around Andrew a lot lately. I wonder why, though. He does have two older brothers. Now both Harry and Andrew laugh at me. I hate them.

Tonight I sat on Andrew's lap again watching television. "Mom" and Daddy were out. It was dark except for the glowing television screen. Andrew was kissing me and using his tongue. It's kind of nasty but he likes it. He also pets my body and hugs me. Sometimes I can feel his penis getting big under me. I'm not sure I like it but I'm not sure that I don't. The biggest problem is that Andrew's my brother, well, stepbrother, but still.

October: I can't understand what Andrew fights about with his mother but now I am fighting with her too. I am always being punished for talking back, not cleaning up. She scares me sometimes. I know I can be insolent but she seems crazy. She's happy and then suddenly she isn't. She stops talking and I can feel a little frightened. I figured out if I don't say anything and wait awhile, sometimes, but not always, she acts like nothing happened. She never wants to talk about it later. In a weird way I'm happy that she doesn't just pick on me. But she never seems to get mad at Guy though.

December: "Mom" got a Hanukah bush. It's really just a small Christmas tree that's sprayed white with blue ornaments. We finally saw Bert and Sally. I don't think "Mom" likes them. She didn't say anything but I feel it. Also I just realized that I am calling her "Mom" not Judy. What would Mommy think? I have to stop thinking about it.

On New Year's Eve I went out with Sue and her family to the movies for the midnight show of "L'il Abner" and "The Jayhawkers." I liked the Jayhawkers better, even though Daddy's friend Mr. Panama wrote "L'il Abner". Sorry. They flicked the lights in the theater at midnight. Whoopee! 1960. Then at 1:30 AM we all went to the Hickory Hut for hot chocolate.

Chapter 16:
Teenager 1960

January 1, Friday: Today our whole family went to dinner with Roger's family. Roger gave me a present, a small gold jewel box. It's okay. But I'm through with him. He's so babyish. Andy was such a nut tonight.

Saturday: Today "Mom" took me to Ohrbach's to buy a bra (30 A) but we ended up at Leed's Shoe store. I got new shoes but didn't get the bra. But it's OK. My feet are growing faster than my boobs. Anyway after dinner I went to Sue's and bragged about my new shoes and showed her the present from Roger. (She does have big boobs though.)

Sunday: I stayed home and worried about school because Report Cards are coming in a few weeks. I asked Andy why he's mad at me. He said he wasn't but that I was. False. He's such a phony, I don't know how anyone could like him. Kissing, petting, necking that's his line. I don't have anything against it but if you say you don't want him searching through your clothes I think you have the right to stop it. Then if he doesn't get his way he'll just ignore you. That's worse than fighting. He's sort of like his mother that way.

Monday: Back to school. Today I got a citation from Susie H. for not wearing a full slip. She gave it to me during gym when I was getting dressed. I don't have a full slip. And I'm afraid to talk to "Mom" about it. I am also getting teased for my hairy legs. "Mom" won't let me shave.

Wednesday: When Daddy got home tonight I waited until "Mom" was in the shower then tiptoed into their bedroom. Daddy was asleep under his newspaper as usual. I woke him up and explained about the slip and he whispered he'd do something about it.

Friday: I recited my poem ("The Swing" by Robert Louis Stevenson) in Miss Warder's English class and I made cinnamon pinwheels in cooking class. They tasted okay. Walked part way home with Rachel, my best friend, Anna, Karen and Pat and went to Thrifty's and bought a new pink diary for 1960. Then I took the bus home. Mom's sick with a cold and Guy's girlfriend Taffy (from two houses down) came over for dinner. I walked her home later.

Saturday: I have to stay home all day because Mom's still sick. My loose tooth fell out. I'm going to make dinner so I can get extra credit for my cooking class. Actually I made breakfast, lunch and dinner (hot dogs). Daddy and Mom seemed to be in a good humor. And I made up with Andy. "Markham", the detective show, was on Channel 2 and I was on Andy.

I couldn't sleep much because the hamster was running on his wheel all night. (I have a hamster by the way, my goldfish, Kitty and, of course, Mitou.)

Sunday: I put my hair in two ponytails, one higher than the other. It makes it look longer. I used to always want to have a ponytail. Anyway I called Sue and told her my ponytail is longer than hers, because of the way I put it and she hung up! That's the way she is. And Mom is mad at me again. I really don't know how I can live like this. Every step I take, I do something wrong or I'm doing something not quite right. Most parents would talk to their child quietly (nicely) and explain what they did wrong. And I'm in a fight with Andy.

I overheard Daddy "talking" to the television. I think it was the news that in Utah some people are starting to act like Hitler again - they are going against the Jews. I picked up the hamster. Yay.

January 11, Monday: Back at school. Rachel's absent. I wore my hair in two ponytails but took it down later. The boys laughed at it. And it's pouring rain outside. Andy's still mad at me. He doesn't say a word. What a son of a blank! He wrote in my little black book that I loved him. I'll say. Mom is acting up again and Daddy's on her side. I need some dresses and shoes and need to get my raincoat back from the dry cleaners before I get drenched. Mom thinks I can keep wearing my old clothes that are now above my knees. Everybody kids me about it and I'm going to get another citation. The wool outfit that she bought me last year before they got married (and I started J.B.) is too short and the white buck saddle shoes pinch my toes.

January 12: I wrote a letter to Daddy but I don't know if I'm going to give it him. I wrote:

Daddy,

This letter will probably be the last letter I will ever write to you. Everything you tell me to do and tell me I do wrong or I forgot to do this or I'm not considerate of others is all true. Since Mommy died everything in this household has gone wrong, even when we tried to straighten things out it never really worked. There hasn't been a day yet that I haven't gotten into a fight with you about something or other. When all this happened, Mommy getting sick and dying, you were so riled up you really just neglected us and I guess you couldn't help it. It was just one maid after another and they didn't give a darn what happened. So now, all of a sudden you're demanding all this. Now Guy on the other hand, didn't really realize what happened so things went smooth with him, that's why he's probably so perfect. Now I'm not asking anything I just wanted you to read what I thought about all this, in these past two or three years. I don't think you enjoy living this way because I sure don't. I try my darnest to keep up. But today, Tuesday, I just got sick because I say hello when you walked in but in the next five minutes you walk back in mad as ever (which is natural) saying "why don't you get this for Mom and why did you go out this afternoon when you know she's sick??" But last night I asked if I could go and I said I'd stay if she wanted me to. She said "Yes". You say to help decide what to eat for supper. Andrew already was making soup when I walked in. You call me again and say to do something. All I did was put soup bowls on the table and put glasses (which we didn't even use). Sue was over and just sitting on my bed. Then you ball me out because I didn't feed the cats and start threatening. Truthfully I hate living in this house. Maybe it's me, but there's never been a day of peace and if it keeps up I doubt there ever will be.

Tuesday: I've decided to run for homeroom president and I wrote my speech. I bought a Clark Bar at Nutrition and when I took a bite, my back molar came out. It wasn't even loose. Blood and gum everywhere! But I got 25 cents for it. I got one B and two B minus': my lowest Social Studies grades.

Wednesday: Rachel's still absent. Got a stomach ache and another tooth came out! I wrote a better speech. And Andy is mad at me again. Mom says I have to practice the piano 45 minutes every day except my lesson day and Sunday.

Thursday: When I got home from school I found a new *full* slip, two bras, a blue pullover and a gorgeous shirtdress (beige and green). It has my initials on it (G.A.). They were all lying on my bed. I guess Mom's not mad at me anymore. I said "Thank you." but she didn't say anything. It feels odd but I do like the clothes.

Friday: Rachel's still absent. And I lost the election, so I ran for vice-president, I lost that too. I finally won for Roll Secretary. Imagine that. I got a 96 percent on my Math test though.

Saturday: After my piano lesson, Sue and I took the bus to Hollywood Boulevard. I got a shrunken head (fake), a rain cap, lipstick blotting paper, three red licorice sticks and a Personal Romance magazine. I spent all my money. After I got home, Mom and Daddy went out for the night. Five of Andy's Hungarian friends came over and walked in my room just as I was pulling up my jeans. I was so embarrassed. Then Sue came over and we all danced to Daddy's hi-fi. Imre, Andy's ugly friend, winked at me. What a thrill… Ugh! Later after everyone left, Andy and I "watched" "Sergeant York" on TV till one o'clock in the morning. He asked me if I loved him but I didn't answer. I kissed him goodnight and went to bed. My stomach hurts (not a baby!) ha ha.

Sunday: Woke up and found my goldfish floating in his bowl. He was almost two and a half years old. Called Sue and we decided to have a picnic and a ceremony for my fish. After I hung up Mom decides that we (all of us) should go to the movies. When I called Sue back to ask if she wanted to go she hung up on me. (She changes plans all the time and sometimes doesn't even tell me…) I called her back and she said she didn't want to go. We went. We saw "Operation Petticoat." It was good. I buried my fish later. Guy helped. It was the first funeral we'd been to.

January 18, Monday: Rachel's back. Finally.

Tuesday: Today we had the State Test. I hope I pass. Then I had a cooking test. When I got home I found Tammy, my hamster, on the floor of his cage. His eyes were open and his head jerked back and forth. I asked Daddy to look at him. He said he was dead. I cried and cried. First my fish and now my hamster. What did I do? What didn't I do?

Mom cut and set my hair for a bubble style – just the front. The back is still long.

Wednesday: I woke up and heard Guy looking for Tammy. I'd put the hamster in a shoe box in the pantry until I could bury him. I passed the State Test. I had my Math final, got my fingers crossed and turned in my Cooking folder. I hope I get a good grade on that too. Got an A minus on my English spelling final. I was surprised that I got an A on my Gym test. Some people at school liked my new hairstyle. When I got home Mom called me a brat because I didn't bury my hamster yet. I didn't because Rachel came over. Daddy started yelling too. I still didn't give Daddy my letter.

Thursday: I buried Tammy. Sue brought flowers. Now Kitty is missing. Mitou is here thank God. I wish he could sleep with me but he's not allowed to come inside anymore.

Friday: After school Sue came over and I was reading her my diary when Harriet called. She asked if her dad could pick me up so I could sleep over tonight and Saturday at her house. Mom said I could. I packed up my stuff and my stamp collection. Harriet's mom is always yelling at her and for good reason too. (Listen to me…) They have a snow white cat and a pure black dog that play with each other. In the house.

Saturday: Today Harriet, her brother and I went ice skating. It was cold. Daddy called. I sold six stamps (plus hinges) to Harriet for $1.25.

Sunday: Today we went to Mt. Frazier. There's snow here and Harriet's dad rented a toboggan. What fun, but my behind got frozen. Brrr it's cold. Daddy picked me up at Harriet's later. I forgot it was Mom's birthday.

January 25, Monday: Back to school. I got a C on my Homemaking test. Report cards are circulating tomorrow. Pouring rain this afternoon.

Wednesday: I've got three A's so far and straight E's. I'm bragging. Sue was absent. There was a Girl's League Installation for the graduates. Half of them were laughing. That felt wrong.

Thursday: I got a B in Cooking and I'm so mad but in Gym I got an A. All E's and A's except for one B! I'm practically sure that I'm getting a Complimentary Notice in Homeroom. My name is second in the hall showcase.

Boy, was Andy friendly tonight. Mom and Daddy were out again. I lay on him and he pushes his penis up and down. It gives me the shivers. He kisses me. There's a wet spot on his pants where I was laying on him. Tomorrow is the last day of the semester and it's a half-day. I wrote Mom a letter saying that $1 is not enough for Town and Country. Everyone is going there after school tomorrow for lunch at Fisher's Hamburgers and I don't want to be the only one that can't eat.

Friday: I brought a few sheets of notebook paper to school. And Daddy gave me another dollar. We mostly signed Burr's (J.B.'s yearbook). After that Rachel, Anna and I went to Town and Country for lunch. Later we crossed the street and went to Farmer's Market and guess who I saw? Shelly R. and is he cute! When I got back home I rushed dinner so I could watch this movie on TV: "Spellbound." I saw it already but it's really good. Did the same with Andy until about 11:30. Mom and Daddy were out again.

Saturday: I had my first piano lesson in two weeks. After that Sue came over and we decided to see the movie "Solomon and Sheba." We were so worried if we could get in as 'under twelve.' It's cheaper but if you're under twelve you need a parent with you to be able to watch this movie. We were by ourselves but we got in. Was it sexy! Afterwards we walked to May Company and bumped into Bonnie. Then we got ice cream at Thrifty's and bought new notebooks for the B8 term.

February 1, Monday: I'm a B8 and today is a half day. I got my new classes. It's a pretty good schedule. I got Mr. Mackintosh for English – woo woo! He's young and cute. And I'm taking Typing.

Tuesday: In Library Science we learned how to check books in and out. Went to Sue's house after school and then came home. Daddy and Mom weren't home but Andy had two friends over. We played records. When Daddy got back he paid me $5 for my five A's! Wow!! And starting Saturday I am getting an allowance, $1.25 a week!

Wednesday: Today Guy is seven years old! I woke up to the sound of snipping scissors. I think Mom was wrapping presents for Guy. Kitty is still missing. It's been almost two whole weeks.

At school all my classes are pretty good except Social Studies. The essay that I wrote turned out to be completely off the subject. But Mr. Harris can't find the papers. I hope he never finds them! Then he'll know I'm a fake - that I really don't understand.

After school I bought Guy's gift, Pick-up Sticks, studied, and then watched wrestling matches on TV with the family. Funny.

Thursday: Well, Mr. Harris found the essays. Just as I thought, I got a D. And on the bottom he wrote "good luck". I'm so disappointed. Now he knows that I'm really not that smart.

Mom took Guy for his check-up at Dr. Goldman's and I stayed home. I was chewing gum and then stuck it on Andy's Spanish homework. I couldn't get it off. Andy blew up. He said, "At least you could say you're sorry". I told him he never did. He said "Sure, sure".

I'm trying to type faster. Thequickbrownfoxjumpedoverthelazydog; nowisthetimeforallgoodmencometotheaidoftheircountry...

Saturday: Had my piano lesson and I think I made Frances, my teacher, cry. Why am such a brat? Anyway Mom and Daddy went to get things for Guy's party. (Only two people showed up.) Diane came over and we met Rachel at her house and walked down La Cienega Boulevard to the Beverly Park & Ponyland. We ate lunch there and watched the little kids bounce around on top of the poor ponies. Later we went to the dime store and Sue ran in and banged the glass on the cosmetics case and almost broke it! She got kicked out. I walked home with Diane. Did English homework.

Sunday: Had to go to Roger's house with the family. He wasn't home, thank God and so the rest of us went to the movies. After, Lou, his father, told us to wait for Roger. I gave Mom a dirty look. I already told her I don't like him anymore. Andy was teasing me. We all ended up eating at Love's together and I ignored Roger.

Monday, February 8: Poured rain all day and we decide to walk home. Soaked, shoes ruined. My hair lost all its curl. Andy called me a "shit". If I could only swear half as much as he... well I don't know. Anyway, I'd say it when Daddy isn't around.

Tuesday: Had a hilarious day at school. Almost tardy, got 100 percent in math, then after class in English, Rachel and I were talking about how much (ahem) we learned today when I said, "Shh shh, he's walking behind you!" The teacher walked up and said, "Hey he's getting close, better quiet down." We all laughed but I was embarrassed. Yesterday, Mr. Harris told us that there would be a surprise in Social Studies class today. Half the period went by with no teacher then suddenly Mr. Harris walked in and, for no reason, sent three boys to Dr. Hunt's office. Mr. Harris was so strict. Everyone was quiet, wondering what was going on. I stared at the clock, twenty minutes passed and then Mr. Harris started to laugh and said that was an example of a dictatorship. The three kids came back from Dr. Hunt's office and then he told us we have to write a 200-word composition on democracy, dictatorship and anarchy tomorrow. We will have a period and a half to write it. I'm writing it tonight. He said not to, but I have to write something!

Thursday: Stupid Erica had to show Mr. Harris her 200-word report <u>she did at home</u>! So we had to hand over our notebooks and take out only two pieces of blank paper and a pen. I think I did pretty well. I tried to remember what I wrote last night. Harris is checking for information and Mackintosh is checking grammar. I got Genevra's telephone number. She's the new colored girl.

Friday, Lincoln's Birthday, no school! Andy's mad at me again, like that's new. Peter, his friend, laughed at me just before I went out with the girls. He's kind of cute, but he has a high-pitched voice, an accent and big red welts on his arm.

I hope Kitty comes back. Please God please.

Saturday: Got Valentine candies and a card for Daddy and Mom. Sue came over and stayed until 11:30. It was real windy. We played "army" and wrote sexy love letters to each other. (She was the boy.)

Valentine's Day: Daddy thanked me for the Valentine. Mom finally did. Wrote my book report then Sue and I went to the trampolines. Then we were supposed to go miniature golfing and Susie S. was going to treat. They ended up going on the tramps twice. I only went on once. Was I mad! But I didn't say anything.

Monday: I started a petition that we request to keep our English teacher Mr. Mackintosh. He's leaving J.B. and we don't know why. After school, I went to the Memorial Library for the first time. Andy drove me. He borrowed Mom's car. It's a public library on Olympic Boulevard across from Los Angeles High School. Inside there's a wall carved with all these names of men, really boys, who died during World War I and beautiful stained glass windows. I checked out a Rogers and Hammerstein piano music book. As soon as I got home, I tried sight-reading "Oklahoma" but Mom told me to stop playing.

Tuesday, February 16: On the way to school, I sang "Happy Birthday" to Daddy. He's 48! Thirty-six years older than me. Wow. I saw him smiling in the rearview mirror. Anyway, the petition didn't work. And I got a C on my Social Studies essay. Figures. Well it's better than a D. Went to get Daddy's cake and an older man opened the door for me at the bakery and then put his hands you-know-where. What nerve! Andy's friend came over and pulled my ponytail. He's nice. And I think Andy has a girlfriend.

Wednesday: Mom blew up at me. She said I made a face at her. She says I always do, which I do not. I wasn't even looking at her. Daddy talked to me after it happened. He said she said she is going to have a nervous breakdown because of me. Huh?

Thursday: We are doing a play in Homemaking and I had an argument with the cast. I think everyone is talking too much. I got my section in my Library Service class: Dewey Decimal number 921, Biography. I really like keeping the books organized. "Cheaper by the Dozen" is on the top shelf.

Friday: I am worried about the play. It's in sixth period. Well, it was awful. I think it's my fault it was so bad. And Andy does have a girl "friend". I heard him talking to her on the telephone. Her name is Annette.

Saturday: Went to the tramps again but this time with Rachel and her younger brother Michael. A girl was jumping up and down doing the "Hully Gully" at the same time to the music playing on the loudspeaker. All the boys were watching her shake her boobs.

Monday, February 22: I'm not sure but I think Andy's girlfriend came over. (I found a pearl with a gold loop attached, on his bed. I kept it.)

Friday: A half-colored girl named Jerri J. asked the boys to feel her up. Boy is she a whore. Sue broke my glasses and she didn't even say she was sorry. I worked in the library after school and found some books about the Nazi concentration camps. The descriptions horrify me. Rachel's and Diane's parents were in concentration camps. They have numbers tattooed on their arms. Rachel said that the Nazi's forced open her mom's eyes while they shot her parents. Nothing with Andy.

Saturday: I had my piano lesson, then went to get my glasses fixed. Mom showed me how to darn socks using a doorknob-shaped thing-a-ma-jig. It's kind of fun. I did two pairs of Daddy's socks and one of Guy's. Went to the movies with the family. Andy was sitting next to me but he didn't touch me. Phooey. I'm such a hypocrite. Maybe I'm a whore too, just like Jerri J.? But it's only Andy and we never take off any clothes. Oh, I forgot, Mom got a housekeeper. Her name is Evelyn, she's colored and older. She comes once a week, on Fridays usually, but she came today. I like her.

Sunday: Raining. I went to the dime store with Sue and bought "Peyton Place". I guess I looked old enough this time.

Monday: Andy calls me an "untouchable". I can't study but I have to. Still no sign of Kitty.

Friday, February 28: The Air Raid sirens went off so we did our monthly Red Alert drill. Five rows of boys were on top of me and one boy off to the side put his hand on my boob. I glared at him and he laughed.

Tuesday, March 29: Mom's going to have an operation. Kitty never came back. I hope she found a better home and isn't dead. I'm sorry.

Wednesday, April 20: Mom had her operation. She had a "hysterectomy". Something like Mommy had, but not cancer. Anyway, I slept over at Susie S.'s house, and now I know my friendship with Sue and Diane is a mistake. Just before going to bed we decided to call Diane. She answered and thought Susie was Bonnie. I was on the extension and stayed quiet. Susie asked Diane about her opinion of me. She said I was a whore and a bitch. Susie S. asked why and Diane said, "Her step-brother Andy"! Guess who told her that? Sue. I didn't make a sound. I called Diane ten minutes later and told her I had just spoken to Bonnie. She gasped. I told her what she 'supposedly' said and Diane swore over a million bibles that she didn't. But I knew. I told her, "You must not be very religious." Then Susie S. started to laugh out loud on the extension. Was Diane mad! But I'm glad. The next morning Susie S. decided to snitch a cigarette pack from her brother. I had one cig and she did too. Well, I didn't like it much.

Monday, May 2: Drurrie is protesting Caryl Chessman's execution. He's supposed to be killed in the gas chamber at San Quentin today. She knows a lot of stuff that I never pay attention to. Anyway, he was executed. So it didn't matter. I made up with Andy.

Monday, May 23: Everything is fine at school but we might have a war!! Khrushchev is threatening the U.S. I French kissed with Andy but what does he care, he has Annette, his "girlfriend." I'm mad at him again and right now I don't think I'll make up.

Wednesday: I passed out birthday party invitations to Rachel, Karen, Anna, Libby, Pat and Helene. Drurrie got sent to the Girl's Vice-Principal's office because she was in a fight. Her ex-girlfriend hit her on the head with her heavy purse. Drurrie started to laugh like it was a joke but that girl hit Drurrie again. What should she have done?? I thought about inviting Drurrie to my party but she's different. She seems older. She's not like my other friends. I like her a lot but I didn't invite her.

Friday: Today Gary L. laughed and smiled at me. Thrill. He's sort of a greaser like Shelly R. and he carries a switchblade! Sometimes he starts food fights in the courtyard turning over garbage cans throwing lunch trash. He gets paddled all the time by the Boy's V.P. (There're two kinds of paddles: one with holes and one without holes. The one with holes is supposed to hurt worse, because it goes faster.)

Andy came to me and said he wants to make up but I think I'm jealous of Andy's girlfriend. I'm just a little plaything when he has nothing better to do.

Friday, May 27: Evelyn was at our house when I got home from school. She's usually quiet when she's here but Mom was still at the beauty shop, so we talked a little. She asked me about school. I really like her.

Mom lets me light her cigarettes. I think she smokes too much.

Tuesday, May 31, my 13th birthday: I'm an official teenager! Yay! Got a transistor radio and Andy got me a straw purse. We had mocha cake and it was delicious. My party is going to be June 18.

Thursday, June 16, Andy's 17th birthday: I got him a "Greatest Brother" trophy. He said he loves me! And he got an old, dark blue Mercury. I think it's a 1954 model and I think his real father gave him the money for it. (His dad lives in New York or maybe in Europe somewhere, I'm not sure. Nobody ever talks about him.)

Saturday, June 18: My party, we had a blast! Mom drove me and five of my friends to Venice beach. We took sunbaths, dug for sand crabs, ate hot dogs, drank soda and jumped in the waves. Later we came home for cake and took pictures of ourselves, in our bathing suits (no polka-dotted bikinis though), in the back yard. I'm burnt and tanned and smell like baby oil.

Monday, July 4, Independence Day: Our flag has 50 stars now. Alaska and Hawaii are officially states but they aren't even "attached" to the rest of the country.

Tuesday: Went with Rachel to see "Psycho" at the El Rey. They won't let you go in after the movie starts. I threw up my Snickers Bar. It was so scary. I'm never taking a shower again.

Saturday: We are building a pool in the backyard!! Yay!

Thursday, August 11: The pool is done and it's slowly filling up with water. I can't wait. It's oval shaped with a diving board. It goes from three and half feet to eight feet. But everything is gone from the old backyard: playhouse, clothesline, incinerator, everything. There's cement all around the pool and Mom wants to change Daddy's workshop that's in the garage into a sort of a cabaña. I wonder if Mitou will be allowed inside when it's done. And she gave away the toy shelf Daddy made me a long time ago. Nope, she didn't ask me.

Daddy asked me a few days ago if I remembered what day was coming. I knew.

Friday, August 12: I got to talk to Evelyn almost all day today. Mom was at the beauty shop for her weekly "do" and said she'd be gone most of the day. It's so easy to talk to Evelyn. She told me all about her husband. He works as a butler out in Malibu. She only sees him on weekends, but she's still so happy. I really look forward to Fridays.

Tuesday, August 30: Well, the 'honeymoon' is over. Andy and I have to clean the pool: every Saturday, rain or shine. We have to brush down the sides to the drain at the very bottom, skim the leaves out, and clean the tiles all around. And we can't use the pool anytime we want either. We can only use it when she's there and we can't invite friends over except on Tuesdays and Thursdays. And only two friends each, even if one doesn't swim. Mom did teach me how to do a backwards dive off the board though. Daddy hasn't gone in yet. He said the bathtub is enough water for him. I don't think I ever remember seeing him swim at the beach or in a pool now that I think of it…

Wednesday, September 1: A woman came over today. I didn't recognize her. She walked in carrying a big square thing with a handle and she and Mom went into the bedroom. The door was closed. This person was kind of heavy and plain. She wore a sort of uniform and had an accent but it didn't sound Hungarian or French. Anyway, Mom didn't introduce me or say anything and after a few minutes I could hear grunting and slapping sounds coming from the bedroom. After about an hour, the door opened and the woman left. Andy told me later that Mom was getting a massage. Weird.

Tuesday, September 6: First day of A8. I was shocked today. I hadn't seen Sue almost the whole summer. She went back East. Anyway, she lost lots of weight and got new clothes. She looks like a grown-up. I saw the boys really looking at her. She says she likes only "older boys" now. I still haven't gotten any new clothes. And I need an increase in my allowance especially now that I have to clean that pool every week. Tonight I talked with Daddy while Mom was taking her shower. I explained to him that I need more money and new clothes that fit. He said he'd talk to Mom about it. Why can't <u>he</u> decide?!

Wednesday: Today Daddy pressed something into my hand that I thought at first was a cigarette! When I looked closer I could see that he had rolled up two one-dollar bills. He didn't say anything to me. I'm happy that he gave me the money, but why does he have to sneak around Mom?

Thursday: When I got home from school I found a white pleated skirt lying on my bed. It's made out of a fabric called "sharkskin". A lot of the girls have them. I like it but it's too long. It can't be hemmed because the pleats are permanent. I'll have to roll it up at the waist and cover it with my blouse and we're not supposed to wear our blouses out... Why can't I buy my own clothes or at least go shopping with her?

Saturday, September 11: Well when I got up this morning I smelled something different and heard strange sounds coming out of the bedroom. Again. Daddy was at work. Andy's room was empty and he wasn't in the kitchen or anywhere else. Guy was still in our room playing. I heard this ripping sound like when I tear fabric, then this patting sound, followed by another kind of ripping sound and then Mom yelling, "Yoy!" Then it would start over. I think it went on for half an hour. Then the door opened and Andy walked out holding a small sauce pan and some whitish fabric. I asked him what was going on and he said he was waxing Mom's legs. Huh? I asked him what he meant and he explained that you melt a certain kind of wax and spread it on her leg with a tongue depressor and pat down a piece of muslin fabric on top, then rip it off. All the hair underneath comes off and is stuck on the muslin. I asked him how long he's been doing this for her and he said, "Awhile". And he does it about every two months. I never noticed before. And she still doesn't let me shave my legs!

Saturday, September 24: I watched the last "Howdy Doody" show with Guy today. And guess what? Clarabell finally spoke. She said, "Goodbye, kids." It was kind of sad. Guy used to watch "Ding Dong School with Miss Frances." Her show isn't on anymore either. But

Sheriff John, Engineer Bill and Captain Kangaroo still are. Sometime we play red light, green light with Engineer Bill. Guy laughs and milk comes out his nose.

Monday, September 26: Diane says we should all watch the Presidential debates on TV tonight. I did and that Mr. Jack Kennedy is cute!

Monday, October 3: Tonight I came in the living room to watch television with the family before I went to bed. There's a new show on called "The Andy Griffith Show." Well when I walked in Mom told me to button my bathrobe, up to my chin. She said it wasn't decent open. I was wearing PJs underneath. I made a face. She sent me to my room.

Monday, October 31 Halloween: Diane and I went trick-or-treating tonight, although I think we're getting kind of old for this. But when we went door-to-door, Diane was telling people to vote for John F. Kennedy! One man argued with her but then laughed because he said she was a good debater!!

Wednesday, November 9: Kennedy got elected and I finally got "the curse" during Social Studies. I was so embarrassed because I was wearing that new white sharkskin pleated skirt that I have to roll up because it's too long and I leaked right through to my desk seat. I had to go to my locker to get my "Emergency Kit". I am the last of my girlfriends to get my period. I'm almost 13 ½ years old. Maybe now my boobs will grow...

Thursday: I got cramps today and Mom got mad at me because I stained the bed sheets. She didn't talk to me about anything. She doesn't get her period anymore because of her operation. She gave me her old sanitary napkin belts. Fun.

Sunday: Sammie Davis Jr. married a white, really white, actress today. He's colored. Nobody colored is supposed to marry a white person. And I think he is Jewish too!! I didn't know colored people could be Jewish either. I don't think she's Jewish. Wow!

Friday, November 25: Today we, Guy, Daddy, Mom and me went to the Fairfax Theatre to see the "Magnificent Seven" with Yul Brynner. It was a good movie with a great soundtrack but the boys that were sitting behind us kept talking real loud and Daddy asked them to please be quiet and one of the boys, who I think I recognize from J.B. punched Daddy in the face and broke his glasses!! I was so scared and embarrassed. It was awful. We left before the movie was over. Daddy's okay.

Sunday, November 27: We, the whole family, took a long drive today and listened to the Radio Mystery Theater on the way back. It was creepy. It was about a puppeteer in a carnival sideshow whose puppet turns out to be a real person. And we also heard the very last broadcast of "Amos 'n' Andy." Holy mackerel.

Monday, November 28: After school Andy, Mom and I went to a place called Brook's Dental Clinic. Andy and I are getting braces. We both need them. My teeth are too big and stick out and Andy has fangs. Anyway they examined us and they start putting them on at our next appointment. It's not a very fancy place. It's not in Beverly Hills. Everyone sits on wooden benches in the waiting room and there aren't any private rooms. All the patients sit in dental chairs right next to each other with their mouths wide open.

December: School's out and Andy drives me with him to the orthodontist every week. We hardly talk to each other on the way there and back. My mouth aches and the clinic has to order special size bands for my teeth because they're so big! This is going to take forever.

Chapter 17:
Left Out 1961

January: I can't remember what's going on. I'm doing okay in school but I want to be better friends with people other than Sue and Diane. Mom's still mad at me most of the time. There's always something I haven't done or whatever. I give up. Guy's going to be eight soon. And Andy's going to graduate from Fairfax next month and hopefully go away to college. That would be good. At least I'd get my room back. I love Guy but I need my privacy. But that's really stupid since Mom's always snooping in my room, my closet, and my drawers anyway. I feel ugly, my braces, my glasses, my lack of boobs, my hair, my hairy legs. I don't even like the sound of my own voice. Oh God I am a mess. Some of the girls are talking about what they want to do when they grow up. That's amazing. I can't even decide what I want to do today.

February: I saw a terrific movie today on Channel 9: "Rebel Without a Cause." I never heard of it before and the boy that stars in it is called James Dean. He's wonderful and he's so cute. And his family in the movie reminds me of mine. I can't wait to see it again.

Andy is going to L.A.C.C. (Los Angeles City College). So he's staying home. Oh well.

March: One of Daddy's business associates named Art Meyer lives near us and we were invited over. I met his daughter Ronna. She's almost three years older than me and graduated from J.B. last year. She's nice and we were talking and I told her about this wonderful movie I saw last month and she took me into her bedroom and showed me this huge scrapbook she made. It's thicker than a phone book! And you know who it's for? James Dean!!! But she told me he's dead. Killed in a car crash over five years ago! I never heard of him until last month. She explained that he only made three movies before he died and it turned out that I sort of saw another one of them: "Giant." That was the movie playing at the drive-in that my real mommy and daddy took us to in Palm Springs on our last vacation together before she died. It's kind of weird. Anyway, Ronna was great to share all her stuff. I think I love James Dean.

I got an Unsatisfactory Notice in French today. I am so embarrassed. I have a French name and spoke French when I was little but I do terrible on all the written work. I understand pretty much everything and my accent is good, but I get D's on all my *devoirs, examens* etc. Sue, whose mom and dad are from New Hampshire gets A's on everything! I feel ashamed that Daddy will see this. He has to sign the notice.

Well, I went up to Daddy's desk where he was sitting and showed him the notice. He said, "What's this?" I explained and he laughed! Laughed. I kind of wished he acted disappointed or mad or something. He said it wasn't that big a deal and not to worry about it. I feel awful. It is a big deal to me.

April: Andy got a long distance call today from Hungary. His grandmother died. Andy was so sad. He cried. She was more his mom than Mom (Judy) is. His grandmother raised him from the time he was a baby until he had to escape from Hungary in 1956. Mom didn't cry.

I found out today that Daddy's legally adopting Andy. Andy told me but he didn't say anything else and Dad didn't say a word to me. Now he will officially have our last name. I wonder what his real father thinks. I don't understand why Daddy is doing this. Maybe it has to do with going to college. I know Daddy doesn't love him. I hope Mom doesn't legally adopt me.

May: I'll be 14 soon, and I'm miserable. Doing fine in school but I wish I had a real close friend that I could trust with all my real feelings. I can't talk to anyone. Sue and Diane talk too much. Everything I tell them they talk about behind my back. So I don't talk with them much. Sue will make plans with me and then if something better comes along she'll go with that person instead and won't even call me and let me know. Some girls at school say that Diane is the most popular girl at school because 'everybody hates her.' They make fun of her and talk behind her back. I don't want to be associated with people who are like that. I like Rachel but her parents are kind of strange. They don't like her associating with me because I'm not "really Jewish". I guess maybe because her parents were in a concentration camp. They don't let Rachel get in German cars, or use German cameras and say she should have only Jewish friends. I'm her good friend at school but not after.

I didn't have a birthday party this year. And I'm punished again, for giving Mom a "dirty look." I'm grounded and lost my allowance for two weeks. I don't even know what I supposedly did or said. But I'm getting real good at pushing her out of my mind. It's either that, I guess, or losing it – my mind. She makes no sense. I feel like I'm tip-toeing around her hoping she won't go off.

I went to Dr. Goldman's for my check-up. I didn't need any shots, thank God, but I did ask him why I have my small pox vaccination mark on my left hip instead of on my shoulder like everybody else. He said he put it there so when I started to wear strapless gowns (!) it wouldn't show. Oh.

June: School is almost over. I'm not going to summer school or camp. I don't think "the family" is having a vacation this year, but I think just Guy, Dad and Mom may be going to Hawaii in August. That's okay. At least I'll have the house to myself. Andy is spending the summer in New York. I'm not sure when he's leaving. He's always out anyway, driving around in his car.

Monday, July 11: One of my cousins came over today. He's really my third (?) cousin, or something, and I've never met him before. He's the oldest son of one of Dad's cousins, Marcella. Marcella's Mom is Pearl. Pearl was Kanka's oldest sister. I don't know her very well because she doesn't live with the "little people." She's very short, though, just like them but obviously she got married. Anyhow his name is Marshall and he's really cute! He lives on the other side of the country in Maryland. I think he's about the same age as Andy. He's staying over tonight and going to the beach with Andy tomorrow. He looks like a greaser and wears a DA.

Tuesday: Morris, one of Dad's uncles, died today, of a heart attack. He was Kanka's brother. There's a funeral tomorrow but I'm not going. Marshall is. I think Morris was 70. Kanka was 72 when he died. They are burying him at the same cemetery.

Now there's only four "little people" left: Philip, Charlie and Pauline. And Pearl. I hardly knew Morris.

August: The family flew to Hawaii for 10 days. Dad left me $20! It's just me and Mitou.

It's usually too quiet in the house when everyone's home but it's a different kind of quiet when she's gone: I'm relaxed, not looking over my shoulder, not wondering what I did or will do that will set her off. And I got a couple of good ideas: I recorded myself practicing all my scales, triads, chords and some of the Czerny Studies on the piano for 45 minutes with my tape recorder; and I shaved the front of my legs, below my knees. Maybe she won't notice.

Rachel and I have been taking the bus down Pico to Venice Beach. (She's fibbing to her mom about who she's going with.) We take the Los Angeles bus to Westwood Boulevard for 14 cents. Then, for 8 cents, we catch the Santa Monica Bus at the corner of Pico and Westwood Boulevard. When we're on the bus, we pass by a cemetery and we have to hold our breath until we pass it. (I'm not exactly sure what will happen if we can't but it's probably not good.) I'm getting a tan and Rachel taught me how to play Gin Rummy and Solitaire. We usually buy lunch from a hot dog stand on the beach. We talk a lot.

I'm trying to write to my cousin Caty in France. She's almost a year younger than me. She's learning English in school and I can sort of write in French. It's embarrassing how hard it is for me though.

September: The kitchen was "remodeled". All the tile is gone, and so is the breakfast room. Mom had the kitchen door removed and hung beads in the doorway (?!). I'm not allowed to go into any of the drawers, cupboards or fridge. Actually none of us, including Dad, are allowed. No cooking either. Why did I have to take a cooking class?

God so much has changed and the worst part is I can't really remember how it was before. Sometimes I wish I could see the future. That way I could be ready for what's coming and I wouldn't have to worry about everything. I remember in grammar school making a folded paper "cootie-catcher" to help me decide what to do. Now I just want to be prepared.

I went back to school. I am now an A9. Next February I go to high school. Whoopee.

October: Dad got a letter from the White House with a tracing of Jackie Kennedy's right foot. She has big feet! Dad said size 10. Anyway, she wants some of the sandals that Dad's little shoe factory makes, the Leilani's. Wow. I wonder how she heard about his factory. Anyway he sent her a pair in every color.

November: It's so warm and dry that my hair's standing on end and I get shocked just touching stuff. Parts of the rich section of Los Angeles, Bel Air, are on fire. I think the fire is near where Mommy and Dad looked for houses a long time ago. A lot of the movie stars' homes are burning and the sky is an eerie orange with ash falling like snowflakes. Today Dad drove us up to see what's left. Just sad looking chimneys and charred trees. I remember the windy, shady streets with no sidewalks. It's amazing how fast things can change. Sad and scary too.

Some of the girls are going "steady." I wish I had a boyfriend. Actually any friend. Rachel is a good friend but even she has a boyfriend so she doesn't have too much time for me.

Today I had a shouting match with Mom and then Dad joined in. It started because I "talked back". I can't even remember what the "problem" was – maybe me balking about cleaning the pool tiles when it looked like it would rain. I was trying to explain to Dad but she kept talking over me. I raised my voice just because maybe he could hear my words. But I got so angry and frustrated that I couldn't think straight and I know I sounded crazy. My words were making no sense. We were all standing in the living room. Dad got angrier and tried to hit me and I dodged him and ran behind the couch so he couldn't reach me. I was so furious, tears were squirting out of my eyes. Dad never caught me. I ran into our bedroom and slammed the door. Thank god he didn't follow me. I am so sad and angry. I feel I'm going crazy. Guy thinks I'm nuts too.

December: I'm getting lots of headaches and I'm always constipated. Mom is taking me to see Dr. Zeigler. I won't be seeing Dr. Goldman anymore. But Dr. Zeigler is nice. He reminds me of Bert. He's kind of a quiet older gentleman. He has a German accent like Bert, and he even came to the house to examine me when I had a real bad sore throat a few months ago. Dr. Goldman never came to our house. Not here or Pasadena.

Chapter 18:
You Are Missing To Me 1962

January: Today I went to see Dr. Z. at his office on Pico Boulevard. It's not like Dr. Goldman's office. I think it must have been a little shop or something before he moved in. You walk in and there are some folding chairs, a wooden floor that creaks in certain places and a big heavy curtain that divides the front of the store from the back. Dr. Z. doesn't have nurses or other people working with him either, just his wife. She has an accent too.

Mom drove me and came in the back with me and explained to Dr. Z. what was "the matter" with me. After a while Dr. Z. asked her to wait on the other side of the curtain. He quietly asked me a bunch of questions and examined me. I told him I get headaches all the time and I'm constipated a lot. Well, I'm going to have to have my head x-rayed and do some test with my nose but not here. I have to go to another doctor. After Dr. Z. gets the results I'll see him again. And he told me to drink more water.

Well, I'm almost finished with J.B. Not too sure about going to high school. I'm used to J.B. now and wish I could stay here. Also I keep changing my mind about which high school to go to. Our neighborhood has a choice: Fairfax or L.A. High. Most everyone is going to Fairfax. That's one reason why I might go to L.A.

And then there's grad night. A lot of the girls have dates. They are all going to go see "Westside Story" at Grauman's Chinese Theatre. Even Rachel's parents are letting her go out - with Steve (he's Jewish). Nobody's asked me. I want a boyfriend so bad.

February: I went for the x-ray and the nose test. Today I went to Dr. Z's. He talked with me and Mom and explained that there was nothing "abnormal" with my head. Then he asked Mom to go wait in front. Dr. Z. didn't examine me but he told me that he thought that I might be getting headaches and being constipated because I am worried. Then he looked up and motioned towards the curtain. I think he was trying to tell me that my mom was worrying me.

I really like Dr. Z.

I graduated J.B. Mom got me a wool suit for the occasion and the same one for herself, different color though. We were twins, except I have braces, brown hair and no boobs.

I decided to go to Fairfax High. Chicken.

I watched Jackie Kennedy give a tour of the White House on television. She's so pretty and she sounds breathy like Marilyn Monroe. I did look at her shoes though. Just checking to see if she was wearing sandals. Ha ha.

March: Fairfax is big and confusing. We have to "rush" for classes, use a "dope" sheet: a long list with all the subjects and room numbers but no map. And I don't even know where the classrooms are. Help. But it's a nice-looking school and there's a beautiful foyer. It's called a "rotunda" with a huge statue of Abraham Lincoln standing in the middle.

Dad still drives me to school – with Sue and Diane. It's okay. But I wish it was just me and Dad. I walk home every day. It's about two miles. And most days I'm hanging around Sue and Diane. I need to make new friends. I also need a new bra. My boobs have finally grown, not by much but I'm getting a red mark around my chest and back because my old one is so tight. I really don't want to ask Dad about getting a new bra.

I finally talked to Mom about the bra. She gave me two of her old ones... Why can't she give me money to buy one or at least take me shopping for one??

Mom took me shopping. Or that's what I first thought. But I was only keeping her company. We weren't shopping for me. She had bought a mink stole from the May Co. last week and decided to return it to the fur department. Actually she "borrowed" it because she wore it to an event that she and Dad went to over the weekend. The sales lady questioned her about the return and I wanted to disappear into the floor. Mom's done this before with fancy dresses but I've never been with her. Ugh. But I did see Marlon Brando!! He was on the escalator right in front of us, wearing a small pony-tail.

April: I am more used to Fairfax but really haven't made any new friends. Sue has been writing songs with Karen and her cousin Edie. They are going to a recording studio on Highland Avenue. They think they're going to make a hit record. I'm writing songs and poems too, though. I'm not telling anyone I'm going to be a star. My first song is called "The Streets of Desire". I wrote the words and the music and can play it on the piano. I'm still taking piano lessons from Frances but I like playing popular music and she only teaches me classical music. It's okay. But I love trying to play the sheet music I borrow from the library or buy from Wallichs Music City. And Mom figured out that sometimes I'm not really practicing the piano even though I'm sitting at the piano and you can hear piano music. Dad laughed though.

I am still pen pals with Harriet and I sent her my latest poem, "The Pregnant Pachyderm". She liked it.

I am writing another called "A Goldfish". So far:

> Your only future lies in a small empty bowl, catching the reflection made in the glass your only goal.
>
> Wandering aimlessly in a monotonous whirl, searching for something - something in the barren, clear swirl.
>
> Not knowing what it is to be able to wish and to pray, nothing to change, to love or accomplish in the coming day.
>
> Alone, waiting, waiting for the time to be fed and to die. Not being able to smile, laugh or be sad and cry.
>
> Just a small, lonely fish barely realizing he is alive. Not even able to leave a mark that will ever survive.
>
> To watch but not perceive, to touch but not feel, a life without soul, a life unreal.

I think I'm depressed or nuts.

I dreamt about Mommy last night. It made me feel happy but I can hardly remember her. It's like she was only ever a dream, I mean, I just have a few photos. I know she's dead, gone, but it's like she was never alive. And I can't really picture myself with her when she was alive. I get why Guy probably can't remember her, but I was ten. I should remember her more. (In my French class I learned one does not say "I miss you" but, *"Tu me manques"*, "You are missing to me.") My mother is missing to me and I think I am missing to myself.

I hate my friends most days, and then I like them. I know I have a temper; I'm jealous, selfish and so self-conscious. I can't pass a store window or mirror without looking at my reflection and not liking what I see. I am a mess. And I can't make those giggly, excited girl sounds either.

Wednesday, April 18: I feel guilty today because I stayed home for some Jewish holiday. Everyone, and I mean everyone, is Jewish at Fairfax, even most of the teachers, so they basically close down the school. There are just a couple of colored kids, Jimmy Soo, and me. I could have worked in the Attendance Office for the day but I decided to stay home. Dad didn't care. He doesn't believe in God or religion. But I still feel guilty.

Saturday, April 28: I went out with Sally and Bert today. They picked me up for lunch. I was so happy to see them. Their son Howard is almost finished with high school and he graduates Hollywood High in June. I think they're proud of him. I felt a little shy but I was so happy to be around them. Dad and Mom don't go out with Sally and Bert much anymore although Dad sees Bert at the shoe factory because he still works for Dad.

Monday, April 30: Mom had pyorrhea (gum disease) diagnosed today. She might need gum surgery. I hope she doesn't have to.

May: Well I'm finally able to appreciate the "scenery" at Fairfax. There's this boy that I call "Blondie" that I have a crush on. He doesn't know I exist. I don't know his name and I try to find him every day. He's not a tenth grader. I think he's in the eleventh grade. He is so cute!

I am babysitting! Sue usually sits for this family but she couldn't so she gave them my number. And Mom said I could. Well, the first time I babysat was a Friday night. The father is the cantor of the local Jewish temple (!) so while the mom and dad went to temple I watched their two kids. They're about five and eight years old I think. Anyway, after their parents left I walked into the kitchen and found that a burner was left on so I shut it off and the older kid started crying and said that now they wouldn't be able to cook on Saturday (??). I quickly turned it on again. Sheesh. Some Jewish people can't do anything after the sun goes down on Fridays and all day Saturday until sunset. Anyway I made $1.50!!! And I'm going to sit for them next week too! Dad said I'm like their *"shabbos goy."* A what?

I can't stop thinking about "Blondie." I got called out by my French teacher for day-dreaming and I got a 20 (out of 100) on a test. I think I'm going to get another U notice in French and one in Science. Help! I had a good dream last night though, woke up happy but I can't remember it. And I'm going on a diet. I weigh 119 pounds! I need to lose nine pounds. I bought a paperback book, "Summer and Smoke" and I read the whole thing before I did my homework. Mom went to the dentist, her gums hurt again. And we had T.V. dinners again. I wasn't hungry and didn't eat. I am listening to Duke Ellington. He did the soundtrack for the movie "Paris Blues" and I really like the music. It's relaxing and full of energy, all at the same time.

Started thinking about how much I always talk and gossip about the people I hate or dislike and never talk about the people I love. That's the trouble these days: no one ever says a good word anymore. I need a boyfriend because listening to passionate jazz and having these weird dreams (and day dreams) isn't helping the situation any. It's like showing a marijuana cig to a drug addict who needs a fix – but you don't give it to him. Oh I am so messed up…

Saturday, May 19: Well the day started okay. I had a good piano lesson and then I was going to go downtown with the girls to look for a dress for Sue. But Mom punished me for something. I think I left a spoon in the kitchen sink, I don't remember. Anyway she said I couldn't go but then she changed her mind. But it might have been better if I had stayed home. We, Sue, Diane, me and two other girls took the bus. I had to be home by 4:30. They didn't, so I took the bus home alone. I got kind of scared on the bus.

Sunday, May 20: I must have gotten out of bed on the wrong side today. What a lousy day, everything went wrong. First Mom got mad cause I didn't offer to clean the pool, but she said yesterday and again this morning, "Not yet" because something in the pool just got fixed. So I didn't. Then Dad asked me to finish a drawing for his work (it will be an ad for sandals, with a sketch of a shoe and a woman). After I finished, Sue asked me to walk to the dime store. Came home, saw Mom standing in the driveway and I asked her if I could spend some more time at Sue's. She was real sarcastic but said "Yes." I came home a couple of hours later and no one was home. No note either. They evidently went to dinner and a movie. Hell! When they came home Dad thanked me for the drawing. Not more than 10 words were spoken between the three of us. I went to bed disgusted (and hungry). God help me.

Monday, May 21: Mom is giving me the silent treatment again so I have decided to write her a "kiss-up" letter. (She had to have two of her teeth pulled and she definitely needs gum surgery.) The letter:

> Dear Mom,
>
> I have never written you a serious letter before and I think now is a good time to write one – for I can't talk too well on the subject. First of all, you're right about everything. I don't know if you'll understand this or not but Saturday (which is a good example of practically all the other problems we've had) I was all set on going then when Freddy and Lisa were coming I knew you were needing help – it sounds awful – but I thought it would be alright to go after you punished me in the morning. After I called Sue I was fighting with myself whether to go or not and as usual I made a wrong decision and went. I thought at the time there would be nothing to help you with during the day since you were cooking. I came home and I thought everything was okay but I see now it wasn't. I thought I was being helpful by washing all the dishes and setting the table. But it seems everything I do is never quite right.
>
> My trouble is I can't make good decisions. Sunday I thought no one was cleaning the pool because of the rubber that was put in – then before I knew it you were cleaning the pool while I was drawing Dad's flyer. It was too late. I came out offering to wash the pool tiles but I guess that was the wrong time too. So then again I made a stupid decision and went with Sue to the dime store and *again* when I was coming home about 3:00 and saw you driving off – I started crying. Because I thought you left me on purpose. Then when Andy came home I heard you went out so I had dinner by myself.
>
> I always think maybe there's something better for me if I do this or this or whatever it is – because, I guess, cause I'm selfish. It never turns out anyway.
>
> You get me lots of nice things and are real nice to me and then when you want a little something in return I goof it all up. I see your point but it's not helping me. I'm always the same, I always goof everything up, not only with you but with all my friends. When I'm in a fight with you, I always turn to Daddy. He never seems to know what's going on anyway. He's such a softie and I always turn to him but that's no good. He should

be like you. I should have been disciplined a long time ago – maybe this wouldn't have happened. I only hope that when you read this letter it's not too late.

You say when I cry it's my way of saying I'm sorry and all that junk but I'm only sorry for my bad self. I really don't know how you're able to put my clothes away and make my bed some of the time anyway.

I bet if I were half-way decent I could save you a pack of cigarettes every day. I'm not writing this to make you feel sorry for me or anything. I just wrote and don't ask why. I think I've worn out the words "I'm sorry."

Love, Me

(Forty years later, while emptying out the house after she died, I found this letter in the top drawer of the night table, next to her bed. Discovering it there, felt unnerving.)

Wednesday, May 23: Well the letter worked! And I'm in love with "Blondie" again. Mom took me shopping tonight and bought me two (!) bras, size 36 A. I wish the boob part would grow. Things are getting better with the girls but who cares when there are boys!! Oh, I passed the French test. Yay.

Thursday, May 24: Mom got me two pairs of capris and a Dr. Kildare shirt. Mom's so sweet.

Friday, May 25: Mom gave me another top. Wow. I might have to write her another letter… They, Mom, Dad and Guy, are going to San Ysidro near Mexico tomorrow for the day. Business. (Dad just opened another shoe factory there.)

Saturday, May 26: What a crazy day: freedom from parents. Whee!! I got $25 in the mail for my birthday from my great uncles Philip and Charlie and great aunt Pauline. Went shopping with Sue and Carol in Beverly Hills and came home to a wonderfully quiet house and made a cake. In the kitchen. I ate two pieces. Then Sue called and asked me to come to a "social." Well I didn't know for sure what time Dad, Mom and Guy were coming home. Then Mom called and said that they were returning tomorrow (!) and to make myself a TV dinner. But then there was another call from Dad's business partner in San Ysidro saying they were coming home later tonight. I didn't know what to do. I decided to go with Sue and I had a blast. We were the life of the party and a guy, Bob, asked me for my phone number!! We were holding hands and all that junk! We, Sue and I, not Bob, came home and they weren't back yet. Sue slept over.

Sunday, May 27: We ate cake for breakfast, and then studied "Julius Caesar." Family came home later. What a great weekend!

Monday, May 28: Well, Bob didn't call. And I've been worrying about Saturday night and going out on dates. Help! What am I going to do? I want Bob to call but if he does and asks me out, Mom and Dad won't let me go out. Anyway, Mom took me shopping for my birthday present. I wanted a black leather jacket (don't ask...) and squaw boots. We went to a dozen different stores but didn't find them. I pouted. Hell, I'm so selfish.

Tuesday, May 29: I'm giving myself one more week with my "Blondie" crush. Today I watched this girl walk up right behind him and grab him by the neck. He turns around and says jokingly, "What ya want Janet?" then she turns around and walks away like nothing happened! I'm sure he noticed me standing there. One more week and that's it. Oh, Mom got me the leather jacket and some white boots that didn't fit. I want black anyway. Now all I need is the motorcycle. Dad didn't appreciate my jacket.

Wednesday, Memorial Day: It was nice not having school today. Bert and Sally gave me a really beautiful beach towel for my birthday.

Thursday, May 31: Well I'm 15 and I don't feel a bit different. I think I'm giving up on "Blondie." It's hopeless. I dreamt about Jimmy (James Dean) again. Mom got me a couple of dresses and two cute pairs of PJ's. Guy gave me his Flintstone's game. He's so sweet. Andy gave me a record.

Sunday, June 30: I spent the last of my $25 birthday money on a sweater, a blouse and a record. Not much happening in the boy department except one of my stepbrother's friends asked me out a couple of weeks ago but I ducked out. I finally got accepted to the BBG's, (the B'nai B'rith Girls) the Jewish temple's social club for teenage girls. I don't know why it took so long. I didn't tell them I was Catholic, well, baptized Catholic (I don't go to church anymore). Dad and Mom are sort of Jewish. Maybe because they're not religious, they never go to temple or anything. Anyway I was accepted and went to two so-so socials. Oh, by the way I am now *allowed* to go to socials but I have to be home by 11 p.m. Nothing ever happened with "Blondie." I almost completely forgot about him except that two days ago I dreamt about him. Now I miss him but there's always summer school, which I really don't want to go to.

I got a new red one-piece bathing suit to match my period that I just got this morning.

Wednesday, July 3: Summer school is okay. I just hope I pass my classes; I have to. Looked for "Blondie" but didn't see him. I think about J. Dean more and more and I compare myself to him when I am so confused about everything. I have to keep busy or I'll go nuts. I am always asking myself, "Is this right or wrong?" and "What's going to happen?" I'm crazy, I must be. I have to love someone, someone I can touch, feel but love most importantly. Someone real, alive.

Wednesday, July 11: Well I finally saw "Blondie" at summer school, cute as ever but he didn't notice me. Classes are all right. What should I do with my hair? Help. I bought two magazines about J. Dean today with lots of great photos. He means so much to me. Why? I don't know. I must love him in a "sisterly" sort of way. If one wish could be granted, I'd ask that Jimmy and Mommy be brought back to life.

Tuesday, July 12: Today I had my first cavity filled in my entire life. I got lost trying to find the dentist's office. Boy was the cavity huge.

Saturday, July 14: Had a good piano lesson then got my hair cut. It looks alright, I think…I went out with Sue's gang later and had a miserable time. I'd rather not think about it. I did borrow "East of Eden" from the library. It's very good. Well anyway, Andy is acting real friendly – you know the sort of friendliness that makes you uneasy. There was a social and I met this real cute, short guy but he had to leave early. He was a very good dancer. Then this other guy kept pestering me to dance, so I did. The boys actually fought over me! Then I had to go, it was getting close to 11 but Sue didn't want to leave because her cousin Edie wasn't "attached" yet. Well anyway the boy named Dave that was pestering me, had the only car so he drove me home with Sue. He walked me to the door and I kept talking. I couldn't find my keys. Then I rang the doorbell and Andy, half naked (he just took a shower), answered. No kiss, but Dave got my phone number. I'm so confused.

Sunday, July 15: At first today I was going to stay home but I decided to go with the gang (Sue, Diane, Carol, and Edie). I think I looked pretty good. We went to the Pancake House for dinner and met up with two of Edie's boyfriends. When we were done eating, they drove all five of us around. We were crammed in like sardines. And we ducked every time the cops went by. Then we drove somewhere in the hills where the oil wells are. It was a steep, winding road not meant for cars. I was sort of scared but I had an out-for-kicks feeling too. One time the car started rolling backwards down the hill, but Edie's boyfriend hit the brakes just in time. We goofed off where the props to the movie sets are. It was fun until the cops came, so we left and bummed around at this guy's friend's dump. It was his house but it was so filthy a pig would have trouble getting used to it. Anyway I got home safe and sound and on time. Dave called while I was out and I guess Dad gave him a hard time on the phone. I'm mad at Dad. I'm not marrying this guy...

Monday, July 16: I was supposed to come straight home from summer school because Mom had another one her operations for her gums. I didn't really come back that early but she was too sick to notice. Guess what? I am allowed to "cook" in the kitchen. At least until she feels better. I made TV dinners and tapioca pudding. Dave called again and asked me to some 'installation' tonight but I said I couldn't. I was telling the truth. I couldn't because of Mom, not that I wanted to or anything. It's so strange how much friendlier everybody seems when you have a boyfriend. And I don't know if I like him or not. I'm so confused about everything. I want to find out what life is all about. I wonder if I'll ever become anything. Oh what the heck.

Tuesday, July 17: I'm doing pretty well in my summer school classes, especially Algebra. And I've been hanging out with some other girls, Pat and Simone. Maybe I'm slowly leaving the "main group." I ate lunch at Thrifty's with Pat and we met Carolyn and Marla. (They were part of the "popular group" at J.B.) I felt so confident today. Oh, Simone said the installation was great. Darn. Dave didn't call but Andy was on the phone half the night, so maybe he couldn't get through. Mrs. Spiro did though; I'm babysitting Thursday night. Money, money, money. Dave better call. Everyone seems to be acting so much nicer.

Wednesday, July 18: I was sort of in the dumps today. I did get 100 percent on my Algebra quiz but I think I didn't do too well on my French *examen*. I walked home alone today but I bought "To Kill a Mockingbird" even though I haven't finished "East of Eden." I'm trying to understand the theme of "East of Eden;" haven't figured that out yet. And Dave didn't call again. He better call tomorrow before I go babysitting. Oh I finally told Mom about the babysitting job. And she's feeling better. Sue, Edie and Diane came over tonight – they probably had nothing better to do. But Diane stayed longer and I showed her my baby album. After her dad picked her up I put the photos away but I kept some of my mommy's love letters that I found. I'm going to try and read them. (They're in French.) Oh well, I don't know what's bothering me now, I should feel perfect. Something just doesn't click. I wonder what.

Saturday, August 18: I finally went out on a date with Dave. He came over the next day and I gave him the brush-off and haven't heard from him since. I did have fun that night, but not with him. I met another guy, named Larry. He should call any day now. Summer school is over: I got an AEE in Algebra and a BEE in French which I am very happy with. I've made a lot of new girlfriends, and Rachel and I are calling each other again. Boys seem to be able to talk more easily with me. (Or maybe I can talk more easily with them...) Thank God. But I still feel like I'm running around in circles. I very desperately need someone I can trust and love, even if it has to be a girl for the time being. Also I have many two-faced friends. But I already knew that... I'm happy at moments thinking I'm the luckiest person in the world and then turn around and I find it really isn't so. I'm so confused. I still go to sleep crying sometimes, hoping I'll wake up in someone's arms but I always wake up and find nothing. I know I'm so foolish but I can't help it. It's just like a movie on TV that's gets interrupted by an unexpected commercial. At least I'm not as depressed but I still go mad thinking about James Dean and Marlon Brando. I don't know if that's normal or okay.

Mom is just one of those things you have to live with, nothing more to me. I think. I contradict myself so much. How can I ever really know what I feel? It's empty inside. I just don't know. And when I start talking about what might happen in the future (eight or ten years), kids think I'm crazy to even think about it. Am I?

Oh, Marilyn Monroe's dead. She supposedly killed herself two weeks ago. I was sort of stunned. Poor girl.

Sunday, August 19: I had a long discussion with Sue about life and boys. I'm so worried: am I loved? I feel so left out of it – our family especially. It doesn't feel normal, our family. One time, I told Mom that love was the one thing that doesn't cost money and she said everything costs money, even that! It doesn't, does it? I don't think so. I don't feel that I am loved. I probably am but why don't I feel something?

Tuesday, August 21: One of my newer friends, Brenda, wanted to go to the movies but I decided to say no and save money. I stayed home and watched TV: old movies, love stories.

Tuesday, August 28: I went to Tempo's, the used record store next door to Dome's drugstore across from Fairfax High. I went there about a month ago wondering if they had a copy of "A Tribute to James Dean", an LP album. Well, I got a postcard yesterday that said they found one!! I almost jumped for joy. I'm crying right now. I don't care what anyone says or thinks. I love J. Dean.

I guess I'm bored, wanting school to start again. Sue says these are the best days of our lives. Are they? I don't want to act unnatural towards people – I want to act like me. That's all. But who's me?? I don't think I even know myself. And I don't think it's normal for a person my age to feel this way. Harriet wrote and said that my feelings about love are like Pearl Buck's. Who is she? I wrote Harry back and asked her. And I'm thinking again about changing high schools – just to get away. Or run away.

Wednesday, August 29: I had a pretty fun day. I slept really late, and then Harriet and her mom came over. We haven't seen each other in quite a while. She has changed a bit since I last saw her: she's skinnier, with longer, nicer looking hair and easier to get along with. Maybe it's me. Anyway they took me out to lunch at Van de Kamp's at Prudential Square. I hadn't been there in a long time. After lunch we went shopping at Ohrbach's. I was a little bored but I did find a real cute blue sweater for $6.69. I've saved $1.05 and I'll get $3.15 Friday, so that'll make $4.20. By next week, I'll be able to buy it!

Got home about 4 p.m. and started drawing a large portrait of J. Dean. It looks just like him. And I've played that album so many times I'm afraid I'll wear it out.

Tomorrow is my last piano lesson with Frances. I'm not sure why but I'm really sad. I hope I get a nice, new teacher, not that Frances wasn't the swellest, but I want one just like her. I made some apple crumble for the occasion. Oh, Harriet said Pearl Buck is an author. I guess I'll have to read one of her books.

Thursday, August 30: My piano lesson was quite awkward. We ate the crumble but it turns out that Frances will be coming back one more time on Tuesday.

Monday, September 3: We, the family, not Andy though, went for a two and a half day vacation. At first we weren't sure where we were going but Dad drove north and we ended up in Santa Barbara. We stayed at a nice looking motel, well nice looking on the outside, the inside was a different story. Anyway, the main part of the city is really beautiful, cultured and traditional and very Spanish looking. All we did was eat and sleep with a few 'interruptions.' We went to the beach, went on a boat tour and then I went on a 'swim-o-cycle' with Guy. There was this city guide in the motel room that had a calendar of events for the week. There's going to be a car race on Labor Day. I met no boys but got whistled at many times. Or maybe Mom got whistled at. Anyhow, I ate too much and since they served mostly seafood (shrimp and tuna sandwiches are the extent of my fish delights) I ate several shrimp Louie's and fried shrimp with French fries. It seemed like we ate every hour! I'm starting a diet tomorrow.

Tuesday, September 4: Mom had her last gum surgery today so I had to stay home with her but I didn't want to go anywhere anyway. First I ironed, then I cleaned the pool, then I escorted Mom to the dentist and I waited half the day for Frances to show up. She finally did at 4:30 with a cake. It was so fast – I hardly had anytime to say "boo". The end of an era, five years. Mommy almost could have met Francis. Five years.

Mom gave me 50 cents for no reason! If I stay home until next week I'll have almost seven bucks!! Sue came over later and we played Careers and I told her a whopper, a plain ole lie. It was about a car race and a boy/man I met in Santa Barbara. I did it because I didn't want to feel left out.

Wednesday, September 5: I forgot to mention yesterday – it was actually such a small thing but it made me quite happy. When Sue was over she picked up the picture I drew of J. Dean and was just looking at it. I don't know if she was admiring it or not but she was looking at it for a long time, thinking I didn't notice. She didn't say anything though.

I also found out the name of my new piano teacher: Pamela. I hope I like her.

Today I cleaned out my clothes closet and I have an awful lot. I don't know why I always think I don't have enough clothes or hip ones. And what little Sue has, I'm always jealous of. Those are the things that shock me about myself. And I am too self-conscious! How can I cure that once and for all? I always start fiddling around with my hair or something because I don't look right. I also wish I had will power to do things that aren't that pleasing such as dieting, letting my nails grow, practicing the piano, and my many chores.

Thursday, September 6: Mom's a lot better. After dinner I went to a social and I felt I looked pretty good. There was this guy named Shel who all three of us were vying for. I danced with him three times, but he was interested in everything and everybody. Oh well, there's another social tomorrow. I also have an orthodontist appointment tomorrow. I have to go with my "dear" stepbrother. Puke. Oh well, "laugh and be happy" – that's what Sheriff John says.

Saturday, September 8: A rushed day: got up late, practiced, ate breakfast and packed a lunch. The gang went to the beach. I should have stayed home. Ugh, it was lousy and I came home late and got into trouble. I talked back to Mom and she slapped me. I almost slapped her back but didn't. And Dad and Andy had a fight too. I'm not sure what about but I wish he wouldn't fight with Dad. Dad gets so upset. (They were shouting at each other, no hitting.)

Sunday, September 9: All's quiet on the Western Front at least referring to family situations. After breakfast and cleaning the pool I went to the Picfair Theatre with Sue and Carol. I was squinting the whole time and I still have a headache. (I don't want to be seen in glasses even in the dark.) Carol is a lot easier to get along with but I find myself always thinking before I say anything or do things around her. I don't know if that's right or not.

I was sitting here in an empty house waiting for Dad, Mom and Guy to come home. Sue called and asked if I wanted to walk down to Pico and have pizza. I said yes and left a note for Mom. (Down to $5...) On our way back home, we ran into the whole family, Dad, Mom, Guy and Andy driving to dinner. Sue and I got into the car and Mom was mad. I could tell right away. Anyway me and Sue didn't eat and she came back home with us. We played Careers again. Oops there goes the phone. Well that was odd. Some guy (Nate) from the social just called wanting some girl's (who I don't know) phone number. How did he get my number?

Monday, September 10: Well I blew all five bucks – on red tennis shoes, Keds. (I used to have a pair like them when I was little.) And a purse I'm not sure I want or need. Mom took me. I also got a white sweater like my red one. I guess I should feel grateful for that but I actually felt sort of mad. Mom led me to the purse rack, showing me different purses to pick out. Then I found one and pulled out my money, hoping and thinking Mom would pay. She didn't. I was short

50 cents and she embarrasses me in front of the saleslady. She wouldn't pay the difference. I had to go back to the rack and find a cheaper one. I should have just not gotten any purse. Then we get back home and had an argument over my black leather jacket. I wanted to wear it because it looks good. But she said she's hot so of course *I* can't wear it. Criminy.

This Thursday we register for school. Darn. Hooray? I'm sort of half and half about going back to school. And, yes, I'm going back to Fairfax...

Wednesday, September 12: Today was a bitchin' day if I may say so. I don't have to practice the piano until my new teacher comes. I got some new dresses and a few old clothes from Mom, a post card from Brenda, then went out with the gang. We messed around, walked to Wilshire, listened to "Bye Bye Birdie" and this guy Marty asked me out for Friday night! To go to a movie! Then I looked at next week's TV Guide and guess what I read? "East of Eden," the movie, will be on TV a week from this Sunday! J. Dean is in it! I am so happy! Anyway Marty called and told me we are going to see "The Birdman of Alcatraz" and "Raisin in the Sun." Then he sort of embarrassed me when he cut the conversation by saying, "Would you please excuse me? I need to go to the bathroom." He's not bad looking; kind of funny, a little plump, polite and knows a lot about cars. He drives a nice one too, a white Pontiac. When I called Sue with my "good news" after I hung up with Marty, she was "surprised" that he was taking me to the Fairfax Theater. She "anticipated" that it would be one on Hollywood Boulevard or Sunset, "How cheap." Gosh.

Mom was pretty nice all day but just a few minutes ago she spoiled it by telling me to go to bed and shut off the lights. My bedtime is 11. It's ten to eleven. I'd argue but Mom's always right. She's insolent like a child. Anyway, tomorrow is "rush" (registration) at school. And after, I have to go to lunch with Great-Aunt Pauline...

Thursday, September 13: Well I went to school to register. What an unholy mess. After about two and a half hours I finally got my classes. Sue and the gang were still there after I left. I wonder if I was lucky or I did something wrong. I guess I'll find out. I ate lunch with Pauline. It was okay but she made me uncomfortable when she said she likes this "mom" better than my real mom.

Friday, September 14: Marty called to say he's picking me up at 6:30. I fixed myself up and he came a little early. He kind of surprised me, he looked so good. Anyway I introduced him to Dad and it turns out he knows Andy. Oy. Anyway, we leave and he didn't open the car door for me. I was sort of shocked but kept a poker face. At the theatre, in line, he pulls out a Student Discount card and asks me if I have one. I got uneasy. He seemed like a real cheapskate. (God, I hope Sue isn't right about him.) Then as we're entering the lobby he says, "You're not hungry are you?" and we walk by the counter. Maybe I wasn't hungry but he could have phrased it nicer. We wasted time while we waited for the picture to start. We held hands and feet (our ankles were crossed) but didn't kiss. Then at intermission he left me to go to the bathroom. Again he tells me this. Then he finds out that the show lets out at 11:40 instead of 11:15 so he calls my house. Guy answers and says Dad and Mom aren't home and won't be back until 11:15, so I start worrying. Marty calls his mom and asks her to call my parents later. After the show we drove straight home. Their car was in the driveway. He walks me up to the door and Mom was there. She was real sweet about it. Then he left - no goodnight kiss. I went to bed dog-tired. I don't know if I like Marty or not.

I've been in bed for already 15 minutes but I can't sleep. I pulled up the shade to catch the moonlight. I don't know for sure if I'm happy or not, but it's been a long time since I've felt this content.

Sunday, September 16: Marty called tonight and while we were talking Diane cut in with an emergency call! Ugh! That girl makes me so - well I won't say it. I thought I missed the preview of "East of Eden" because of her interruption but I got to see J. Dean after the Channel 9 Movie Theatre. Is he gorgeous!! I can't wait until next Sunday when it's on. Oh, I almost forgot school starts tomorrow.

Monday, September 17: Nothing interesting happened at school except I saw "Blondie." He is still so cute. I think he noticed me but I don't care anyway. Marty came looking for me after school but I was already home. He called and told me. I had a fight with Mom about walking home with Sue. She says she pays for my bus pass so I need to take the bus. I get home too late. We had one of our "discussions," but I did learn a bit about myself. First, I always think for everyone else before I deal with a problem. Every time I think something is going wrong I always "know" what will happen. I am so pessimistic. Well, that's wrong, I shouldn't be doing that. And I've also built a little wall around myself and I don't confide enough in Mom (!). My thoughts at the moment are being accompanied by a trailing argument between Mom and Dad vs. Andy. He's losing. He's so lazy. To get back to the subject – oh heck, I'm too distracted by this juicy argument.

Tuesday, September 18: Well, another mess of a day. First, we were almost late for various reasons: one being that Dad's car got a flat tire and Diane's pop was late bringing her to our house. Second, we had a French test and I'm certain that I didn't do well but I'm not sure if it counts. Third, I was kicked out of Senior High Art because it's over-enrolled but I filled out a request so maybe I can get back in. Fourth, Fairfax is very, very uncomfortable. I want to distance myself from Sue, Diane, the whole crowd. But I'm afraid to be by myself, and I haven't met any new friends. I know, I know, it's only the second day of school but it's still awkward. And fifth, after school, Mrs. Arkatov called and told Dad the new piano teacher, Pamela, can't teach me after all, but she has another one lined up. So I reluctantly call this new teacher to make arrangements and get information. I hang up and explain to Mom what the arrangement is and she gets mad. This new teacher would like me to come to her house for lessons. She doesn't live too far away, near Doheny I think. Anyway Mom doesn't want to drive me or whatever. So I call the teacher back and she agrees to come here. She sounds nice but she seriously likes to talk. Then Mom says "Will she come over for $3?" I say, "No, because I told you before, she charges $3 over there and $3.50 over here." So Mom gets mad and I get mad because she got mad! Mom had said nothing about price when I first told her. It felt like a carbon copy of last night's fight. So we'll wait until next Friday when Susan - that's her name - comes for the first lesson. Mom will do all the talking. Jeez.

As usual, I guess Mom must have tattled on me to Dad. He tells me I'm too rash. Maybe I am, but she has it in for me before I can even explain. Nothing I do seems to help. Dad looks kind of weary. And I worry way too much.

Thursday, September 20: Our car pool problems are solved, at least my part of it: I'm going with Harry next door. I was tardy to first period because I was getting my textbooks and I still don't have my sixth period class. I didn't go to school with Sue and Diane or come home with them either. I walked home with a couple of new kids. I'm not sure if it's an improvement. I'm a little anxious about my piano lesson with "Susan" tomorrow. Yes, I know. I'm talking myself into a problem.

Friday, September 21: I went to school with Harry again and didn't really avoid Sue and Company but I hung around with about everyone else. I'm happier. This is what I've been trying to achieve for a long time: being able to keep away from them as much as possible while still being friendly. I'm hanging around a lot with Simone and met a new girl, Francine, who just transferred from Hollywood High. And I had my first piano lesson with Susan. She's very good but she's not Frances.

Saturday, September 22: I got my $4 allowance and I walked up to Wilshire Boulevard to meet Simone and a friend of hers. I got there and saw Erica who said she just saw them at May Co. So I go there but I must have just missed them and never found them. I started feeling like everyone was looking at me – I always do when I'm with no one. So I left and went home early.

Sunday, September 23: I have waited nearly two weeks to watch "East of Eden" on TV. It was so GREAT! James Dean is so cute and sensitive-looking and his acting is wonderful. I recorded the whole thing on my tape recorder and Guy manned the telephone. Marty and Simone called; he told them I wasn't home. No interruptions except for commercials. That movie, I can't explain it, it was just terrific and that lucky Julie Harris getting to kiss him. Swoon. If I'd had the chance to kiss him I would have absolutely melted away. I've been having lots of dreams about him and me. Oh, if they could only be true...I'm so glad he existed, I know this sounds corny but I have something to live for right now. Something to make all the bad things good, something to make me try and understand. It hurts me to read all the bad stuff they write about him. I hope they never were true. I'm embarrassed to show my real feelings. That's the trouble, people are such sheep; he was the first actor who was brave enough to do what *he* liked no matter how silly or stupid it was. And now look at how many people are trying to be carbon copies of the image he left. But what's wrong with them, is that they don't feel "it," understand why they're doing it. That's the difference. I want to find someone like him to love forever. Tell me I'm not just a silly girl. Please.

Tuesday, September 25: I'm still "soch'ing" it up with Fran and her crowd. My hair looked good today, and I wore my leather jacket. Carol said she got one too. I got mad. I guess I had no right to be mad but I have to admit I was and still am a little. Oh well, I'll solve it by not paying attention to her. Tried to listen to my recording of "E. of E." but Mom came in and stopped me. Why? I do not know. I had that fight with her yesterday and part of today but I think we "made up". Know why? She needed me to style her wig. Yes, she has lots of wigs, falls, and fake chignons.

Friday, September 28: I'm hanging around a lot with Fran. She's sweet, petite and very friendly. She introduced me to a bunch of her friends. Several kids transferred from Hollywood to Fairfax. Now that I'm an

A 10 I can rush for one of the girl's clubs that are not officially approved by the school, although they still exist. There are four girls' clubs: the Kappa Pi (the sorority types), the Zeph's (the tough girls), the Cubadons (the squares) and the D'Artagns (the rest). I'm thinking of rushing the D'Artagns. We'll see. I'm a lot happier socially, but Mom is ruining everything as usual. She still won't let me use the tape recorder until she feels like letting me. It's mine.

Friday, October 5: Woke up early this morning at 7 a.m. when I suddenly got a call from Brenda telling me they just said my name on KFWB radio, Channel 98. If I call within ten minutes, I win $9.80! She gave me the number and it took four tries but I finally got through and talked to DJ Wink Martindale himself! He said, "Congratulations, you just won $9.80". I was shaking, I was so surprised. People kept calling me to tell me I won and at school people kept walking up to me saying congratulations. I hope I really get that check.

Fran is a good friend. She is so supportive. I don't think I've ever had a girlfriend quite like her. She understands my need to separate from Sue, and everyone else and told me how proud she was that I am making it on my own, not having to depend on others for my happiness. That meant a lot.

I was supposed to meet her tonight at the Fairfax "Sports Night," but then Mom and Dad said that they were going out and I was supposed to babysit Guy. I was so upset. I had told them a week ago that I was going and it was too late to call Fran and tell her I wasn't coming. And I didn't have a way to get there. Then Andy came home and offered to drive me and watch Guy so I hurried to get ready and when I went to say goodbye to Mom, she started sobbing and then real bluntly says "Good bye!" I ask her what's the matter and she says, "Nothing!" As I start to leave she starts babbling about how inconsiderate I am. I go to talk to Dad and he starts yelling at me. So I ended up staying at home, screaming all the way to my room, "Now you can go out!" and swearing under my breath. They never went out! I was so miserable because I knew Fran was going to be mad or disappointed. Then Marty called and asked how come I wasn't there and that he had planned to take me to Pandora's Box on Sunset Boulevard! So I went to bed miserable after a lucky day.

Saturday, October 6: I finally met up with Simone and also got my allowance: $4.50 – a 50 cent increase! I was sure it would be taken away. But Mom and Dad vs. me is still not good. Mom argued with me this morning about cleaning the pool. I told her I would come home earlier to clean it. So I come rushing home at 4:30 to clean the damn pool and they don't come home until 10:30! I was on the phone for about three hours, first talking with Sue for about a half hour and then Fran for almost two hours. She told me lots of personal things. Her mom has breast cancer and Fran *had* leukemia. She took some new medicine and she's okay now but she's very short for her age. I think she's a real friend. I hope that she doesn't disappoint me by talking behind my back or making plans then standing me up.

I had absolutely nothing to eat. Mom and Dad came home and said "Hello" and then "Good night." Boy, oh boy, what a life. I hope things improve with "our" family because right now it's getting on everyone's nerves.

Sunday, October 7: Things are calmer. We'll see. I stayed in my PJ's all day, talked with Fran and decided that I'd like to go out with Marty one more time and then slowly break away. I want another boyfriend. I'd like to go up the ladder a little bit faster. God, I sound like a jerk.

Tuesday, October 23: I didn't know so many things could happen in such a short time. I've been drawing more and more, went on two (!) more dates with Marty, and now I don't like him. He tried to undo my bra last date! I got mad but he's still calling me. And I did get that check!

I decided to rush for the D'Artagns. Fran has to wait until next semester because she's a B10. There are several "rush" activities that I must participate in and I just received the invitation for the first activity. I guess I have a pretty fair chance of getting in but I can't be sure. I'm still best friends with Fran and this guy Rick W. called me. But I think the most important of all is that the US may have a war with Cuba! A nuclear war! We'll know in 24 hours, according to the news. I pray to God that they can settle something. Just about everybody started thinking about all the things that we take for granted after hearing Kennedy's speech. Anyway all we can do is wait and pray.

Wednesday, November 7: Well I was invited to the D'Artagns Tea, and I guess I'm happy about that. I lost $3 a couple of days ago and that led to a chain of events and another fight with Mom. Now everything is calm but Mom's sick with something. I did get a U notice but I am doing better in French. And I went out with Marty, again, but I don't want to go out with him anymore. I'm tired of him. God I was just thinking, I haven't been kissed by a boy in over a year. And if you don't count my stepbrother, it's closer to three years. I seem to have many more new friends now, but I'm slipping in school. I better catch up. I've been thinking lately about the future: college, a career. I tell myself I want to be an actress but I can't tell if that's what I truly want to do and it's so hard to get into "the business." My only real skills are playing the piano and my ability to draw. That's not much experience. I want to go into acting more and more to show myself, some of my friends, and my family that I can do it.

I've also figured out something: I don't really need boys yet (for love, petting and making out) unless other girls are talking in front of me discussing their dates. I just don't want to feel left out, left behind.

Oh, how could I forget! Kennedy spoke on T.V. and the radio last Friday and he said the Soviet missile bases in Cuba are being dismantled. Whew.

Monday, November 19: I got a job! At Eastern Mortgage, courtesy of one of the D'Artagns, but I'm getting sick of it already and it's been only three days. I haven't received my Social Security card yet but I should be getting it any day now.

Anyway everyone tells me that I'm going to get into the club. I don't want to get my hopes up, but I sure would like to get in. My fingers are crossed, another week and a half till we all know.

Only three of us were invited to this private D'Artagns affair; Erica and Edie were the other two. I couldn't go because I had to babysit Guy. He's almost 10 years old!

I went horseback riding with Marty on Sunday for almost two hours. I know, I know I wasn't going to go out with Marty anymore, but I'm thinking I like him again. Anyway, I really like horseback riding. I know, I know: I am a "user". Poor Marty. I am so busy these days but I am not spending enough time on schoolwork. I got a lousy report card: two B's, two C's and a D in Geometry (but I was expecting to fail). I got a BEE in French, though.

Tuesday, November 20: I kind of had a fight with Fran today. We were at Thrifty's. While I was buying some pistachios at the counter Fran kipped some costume jewelry. Her friend Marilyn did it too. Nobody from the store saw. They bragged about it after we walked out. I told her that I wasn't comfortable with stealing stuff. Fran wrote me a note to apologize but it left me feeling weird about her. She told me in her note that she kipped a blouse from May Co. two months ago and promises to stop.

Thursday, November 22: We, the family minus Andy, are driving to Palm Springs for the Thanksgiving weekend. Great Uncle Phillip sold his mansion on Hudson and bought a house in Palm Springs across from Eddie Cantor's (the entertainer). We're staying over for three nights.

Saturday, November 24: I guess I never really knew these relatives very well. They are so wealthy and they're still so unhappy. Maybe that's why they never got married. They are always complaining about something or someone, especially Pauline. We've only been here two days. Maybe they were starving for new blood. Here's a brief sketch: picture my great uncle Philip having an asthma attack and picking his nose, Uncle Charlie spitting, coughing and sleeping all day, and Great Aunt Pauline spitting and talking with a really full mouth. And I get to sleep with Pauline; I'm in bed with her now. Help. I can't wait until we leave, it's really disgusting. Even Mom and Dad think so. I did get to go horseback riding with Guy in the desert yesterday. I had a terrific horse and Guy did very well. We had a very cute guide too, but my hair looked awful.

Sunday, December 2: Well, I made it through the first round of voting for the D'Artagns. We'll see what happens.

Monday, December 3: I quit my job. I felt like a caged animal but now, at least, I have my Social Security card.

Sunday, December 16: I was supposed to be "snatched" early yesterday morning by the senior D'Artagns but Mom wouldn't let them surprise me. Mom should have left the front door unlocked for them to grab me while I was still asleep. But she refused. So they had to ring the doorbell and naturally I woke up but Mom did let me go out in my PJ's, robe, slippers and hair rollers. I looked frightening. They collected all the "rushes" like me and drove us to Hollywood. We were all given rolls of toilet paper and we were supposed to sell individual sheets to people shopping at the Hollywood Ranch Market. There I am, standing in the early morning in my slippers, robe etc. shouting, "Tickets to the Bowl, five cents." I actually sold six.

It was fun and embarrassing. I am officially a D'Artagn. Yay.

Tuesday, December 18: Everyone that rushed the D'Artagns made it. Some of the girls got very upset while waiting, but I knew it was ridiculous to worry. Listen to me. Ha. But, really, other than an iffy status symbol, what is the big deal about being in a club anyway?

As far as boys are concerned, I haven't seen or talked to Marty since we went horseback riding. That's okay. And "Blondie," remember him? Well, he's a real fink. I don't know what that has to do with anything. Anyway, last Friday I went to a BBG social. When I first got there I gave everyone, meaning the boys, the once over. There were about 30 boys and 8 girls. Then I noticed this really cute guy - for an AZA boy. But as the evening went on I realized he wasn't much of a dancer or talker. He seemed different, not so much by looks or actions but I could just feel it. Then after I finished making a spectacle of myself, I was sort of the "belle of the ball," I calmed down and decided to go for him. We sat down on the floor and started to talk about clubs and schools.

Then Bonnie said her mom wanted everyone to leave in about 10 minutes. So I got my jacket and he walked me out. He kind of reminded me of Roger, his physique. He had his arm around me and we got into this guy's car and just sort of rubbed each other, until everyone else got in the car. Since my house is only three blocks away, it didn't take long to get home. While we were still in the car I felt proud, proud that I got this guy. By the way his name is Andy (??). Then we got out and we walked up to the house. Through the window I could see Mom and Dad sitting in the living room, so I stopped at the gate and told him. As I turn around he kissed me. I guess if he hadn't kissed me I would have kissed him. But his lips and mouth were all over mine, it felt so desperate that it scared me terribly. I was really shaken because it was too much, too soon. I hadn't known him an hour and I wonder what he might have done if we had had more time.

I don't remember what happened after he kissed me. I think we said goodbye. I remember opening the front door with a wet feeling on my lips, saying hello to Mom and Dad and walking into my room, and staring into the mirror. He had taken my phone number; he lives in Gardena. I might hear from him once but that will be all. I'll make sure of it. I don't want him. I know what I want and he doesn't have it. You can't judge solely on looks.

And speaking of looks, Diane and another girl Bobbi both had their noses done. A lot of the girls (and even some boys) at Fairfax are having plastic surgery. Fixing my nose won't fix me.

Saturday, December 22: I went to another social, didn't hear from that guy Andy and I don't especially care either. We, the family, celebrated Hanukah this year, not Christmas. I wonder if it's because I joined the BBG. Anyway, Mom got me a pretty mohair sweater, a pair of stockings from Guy, and some unknown record from Andy. I feel so guilty. I can't get anybody presents. I'm broke. Mom also cut off my allowance for next week because I didn't make my bed one time a couple of days ago. I wanted to apply for a Learner's Permit but the fee is $3. Dad gave me his easel and oil paints. I'm going to create something but I don't know what yet.

Its Christmas vacation and I'm feeling very lonely and I'm pretty sure that I won't be going out New Year's Eve. But I did fulfill half of my "resolutions" for 1962: I did go out on a date. Lots of them, actually. Susie S. came over a couple of days ago with her boyfriend, named Marty and this other guy named Andy. (Doesn't anyone ever use their imagination when they name their kids??) Anyway, Susie S.'s boyfriend started fooling around with me outside by the car, picking me up and hugging me. He's not bad looking but he's one boy I better forget about and fast. And Susie S. just received an I.D. bracelet from him, too.

I keep thinking about my career. I want to be famous. Maybe I think that way because I psychologically (whew that's a long word) want people to like me, to approve of me. I am still very confused about life. Every day I learn something new, little or big, and sometimes it helps explain something I'm confused about. But usually I end up more confused.

I'm beginning to wonder why I rushed D'Artagns. It seems like I was rushing a name or a sweatshirt for the status. And I need money. I wish I had a job just for one week. It would really help. But, knowing me, I probably couldn't do it for more than a week.

Sunday, December 23: Guess what? Andy, the wet kisser, called and asked me out to a party today. I told him I couldn't go, but he asked me if I could go next Monday. That's New Year's Eve! I told him to call me during the week and then I'll tell him. I'm still undecided about him and I know Mom and Dad won't let me stay out after midnight.

Thursday, December 27: I got my Learner's Permit! I only missed two questions on the test but God was I nervous before I went. I almost had kittens. Mom took me out driving later. I nearly started crying. But she didn't notice, thank God. I couldn't even start the car! I had been talking so big to everybody about how much I know about cars that I felt ashamed. I went driving on Crescent Heights past Pico about 10 miles per hour. Mom was hugging the door for dear life, and I don't blame her. She asked me to turn into our driveway and I missed it! And then I forgot to brake. I was half way over the curb when I finally stopped. And that was only 15 minutes. Yes, I was wearing my glasses.

Monday, December 31: I decided to not go out with Andy. It's okay; he kind of scared me anyway. So no New Year's Eve date this year but I did accomplish a lot: I did go out on lots of dates, got kissed, got new close girlfriends, became a D'Artagn, got my Social Security card and got my Learner's Permit. It still feels incomplete though.

Tonight I ended up hanging around with eight other girls. I got home early, Mom, Dad and Guy were out and I started hearing strange noises outside in front of the house. I call Mom and she says they're coming home soon. They get home and now you can hear this man swearing at the top of his lungs. I tell Mom what he's saying and she gets mad at me for repeating it! I hardly ever use that kind of language and never around the house; well, sometimes I mumble it under my breath. But still! She's mad as hell – so in the usual tradition I ended up having a miserable New Year's Eve.

P.S. Well, I guess a lot of people on our street had a miserable New Year's Eve too: Dad's, Mom's and practically everyone else's cars that were parked outside got their tires slashed last night!! I wonder who did it. Maybe the man with the foul mouth... Ha!

Chapter 19:
Happy Daze? 1963

January: I was thinking while I was soaking in the tub about why everybody teaches kids to be so hush-hush about nakedness and sex. This constant embarrassment about it just makes it more inviting for some people to be more outspoken. It makes it such a crime when somebody talks about it innocently. And what's so wrong about so-called beatniks that like strange music, "immoral" poetry? Why is it a problem to watch or hear of their antics?

February: I haven't been on any dates since December, and I owe the D'Artagns $12.50. I'm not sure how this club is helping me. All they do is collect dues and plan for the next group of rushes. I had another gigantic fight with Mom. I won't bother with the details. I passed Geometry I and got a BEE in French. This is the year that everyone is turning 16 so I've gone to a bunch of "Sweet Sixteen's" already. They're a big deal. It's almost like a wedding. Every one that I've been to so far has been at a big restaurant on "restaurant row" on fancy La Cienega Boulevard. The party is usually in the banquet room because so many girls are invited and most of the birthday girls want 14 K gold charms to add to their charm bracelets. I'm already worried that Mom is not planning a party for me. And I feel too uncomfortable to ask her about it.

I've changed my mind about acting for one reason or another. I guess mostly because I haven't had any opportunities. I know that I could take (or should take) at least a drama class at Fairfax, but I haven't, probably because I'm chicken. And I feel kind of lost again. Who am I? It may take a lifetime to answer but I'm getting impatient. At least I'm on as good of terms with everybody as presently possible. My hair is longer and I look more surf and moody than ever. I don't know if that's me or the "sheep" in me. I just can't figure out how to "be" – I want to fit in but at the same time I don't want to be like everyone else. Help.

I just started the new semester so I can't tell yet how good or bad I'm doing at school.

As far as boys, I'm okay until other girls start talking about their boyfriends then I begin to feel left out and jealous. But then I think that I feel this way because it's the thing to feel. Deep down I don't think I really care but then again I don't know for sure. Seeing one boy for a couple of weeks, then another, well, I just don't get it. Maybe it's right that you should have "practice with people" but I believe more strongly that the right guy will come along and to let fate do its job. But then again, I don't know. It's so hard to wait. And the other thing that bothers me is the feeling that I'm out of the loop. Not included, not invited, or talked to. Am I normal? I would like to be able not to care when I feel left out but I'm too dependent and self-conscious. One way maybe that I could help myself is to learn from my mistakes and be confident of what I do and say. But on the other hand I shouldn't hurt anyone in doing so. Lastly I'd like to learn the real meaning of being natural, of love, of respect and of security. Oh well.

April, Easter Break: I'm on my first vacation without my family! I'm in Palm Springs with the D'Artagns. I can't believe Mom and Dad let me go. We're staying at one of the member's parent's desert home. (They have two homes!) It's actually down the street from Great Uncle Phillip's house. Palm Springs is so crowded: there are so many kids that it's hard to walk down the sidewalk. Last night we walked by the Bank of America on Palm Canyon Drive and someone poured soap into the fountain! The bubbles filled the fountain then cascaded all over the sidewalk and into the street. What a mess. We're supposed to have a chaperon but I haven't seen her. I think I'm having fun but then again I'm not so sure. My D'Artagn sisters are kind of wild. But Dad sent me a special delivery letter with $20 inside! That was amazing. And he told me to call him collect (at the factory) if I need anything!! Wow.

Sunday, May 18: Not much is going on besides school. With boys = zero. I'm getting that impatient feeling again. There's going to be a D'Artagn party soon and I'm supposed to invite a guy. Who? That's the question. It sort of makes me feel miserable and what's even worse is there's no one I'm even interested in. On a lighter note, I might be taking my driving test within the next week or two. Sue went yesterday, her 16th birthday, but she ran into the DMV man that was supposed to get in the car and test her! He had to go to the hospital and Sue did not get her license. Now I am a nervous wreck.

Dad brought me a guitar from Mexico and I am learning to play. I'm teaching myself and I can play "The House of the Rising Sun" and part of "Malagueña." Mom might redecorate my bedroom. I'm not sure about changing my room but I do appreciate the thought. I still feel very gloomy and depressed down inside. I don't know if anyone can tell, but it's there.

Fran didn't make the D'Artagns. I'm not sure why. Rachel might be rushing next fall but I'm sick of the club. I don't know what it is but I seem to be losing interest in everything. I hope this feeling wears off. I have achieved my social standing among certain girls and boys but I've also reached a dead end. Now what? Before, I had girlfriends to work towards, now I have too many to keep track of. I feel like I've already missed my chance. It must sound ridiculous. But to me, it's feels quite real.

Saturday, May 31: I failed my Driver's Test. At least I didn't run anyone down. I got a 69; 70 points is passing. I almost threw up before we arrived at the DMV but I have another chance to take the test before my learner's permit expires next month. And I didn't have a Sweet Sixteen party. Mom is taking me and four friends to the movies tonight at the Wiltern Theatre. I'm disappointed, but I didn't speak up either. I kept hoping she would think of having the party herself. But Evelyn, our housekeeper, got me a beautiful bracelet! And Uncles Philip, Charlie and Aunt Pauline sent me a portable TV for my bedroom!!

June: Andy moved out and is driving up to Berkeley. He's going to start university there. It's near San Francisco. As soon as he left, Mom moved all of Guy's stuff into Andy's room and rearranged the furniture. I wonder if Guy remembers when it was his room. She's really quick about switching things around.

Saturday, July 6: Well I got my driver's license on the second try (and the very last day of my learner's permit). Thank God. And Sue got into another wreck but nobody was hurt except the car. Actually today is the last day of my four days of freedom. Dad, Mom and Guy went to San Ysidro for business. So me and Mitou have had the house all to ourselves. And I got to talk to Evelyn for the whole day yesterday. I love her. She's such a good listener and I feel normal when I'm with her. She told me, "Honey, you'll make it."

Mom left me the use of the car for driving to summer school and piano lessons but I'm driving all over in her Ford Falcon. I hope she doesn't notice that I've driven 50 miles.

Rachel and I have been going to the beach by bus since regular school let out. Last week on the way back, there was this boy who was standing near my seat that I couldn't stop staring at. I think he goes to Fairfax but I don't think he noticed me. He has dirty blond hair and blue eyes. He's slim and has a beautiful smile.

Saturday, August 3: The biggest news is that I've achieved my goal for the summer: I went out on a date. Fran fixed me up with her steady's, Mitch's, best friend. His name is Mauri. We went out on a Friday night and it was sort of awkward but we made plans for the next day to go to the beach. This was one of those weekends my parents went to San Ysidro. Oh how I love these weekends... It started off a bit uncomfortable at the beach until we got out of the water and were laying out in the sun. He put his arm around me, and well, we got to know each other... He's light-complexioned, has freckles, blondish brown hair, taller than me and a pretty good build. He's a swell dresser, from Uruguay (South America), speaks Spanish and English, Jewish (if that matters any) and is cute. At least I like him. It must have been so funny for someone watching us arrive at the beach and then a few hours later, leave. We walked to the beach about 20 feet apart and "walking" back, maybe if you were lucky you could slip a needle between us. Fran slept over, and Mitch and Mauri came over after work and we (Mauri and I) made out. He's the best make-out. Since then I've seen him about three times a week at school, he's called about four times and we went to a beach party together last Friday night. It was bitchin' – I didn't know half of what I was missing. But since then (a week ago) he hasn't called though I've seen him at school. Fran and Mitch are having troubles. She doesn't exactly know why. Mauri is acting real funny too. It seems that every time I see him I have to start from scratch. It's very hard to converse with him but communication is not always a problem. I sure hope I go out with him again. I love him, I think. He's very nice and is the first boy where I didn't ever have the feeling, "Gee, what will my friends think of him?" (Jeez listen to me. Why do I care so much??) He works all the time when he's not in school, and from what I understand his family is quite well off. He bought his own car, a new Le Mans Tempest. I've lost about 10 pounds since I met him. Christ, I've only known him two weeks and I already want to marry him.

Friday, August 9: Today was the last day of summer school and I got an A in Art (Design) and a B (!) in Geometry II. Normally this would excite me no end but presently I'm very troubled. It's not too hard to guess why: Mauri. Fran and Mitch are back on good terms. Mauri called me last Wednesday night and we talked - about mostly nothing except how he was mad at Fran and then he asked, "Ain't you going to ask why I didn't call you?" I already knew, he lost my phone number but I asked anyway. I've seen him once this week and being this is Friday night at 10:30 sitting at home, I'm obviously not out with him. Fran's pretty sure that I'm going to hear from him soon. I hope so but he's always working. I love him very much. I hope this isn't an infatuation. I think he likes me but he was right when he told Mitch he could never go steady with a girl. He said it wouldn't be fair because he works so much, she'd never see him, which is unfortunately too true. I think that's why Fran and Mitch had their last lover's quarrel: Mitch working all the time. But what Mauri said also means that it's practically impossible for a girl to like him. Since that's not true, I have got to get hold of him. That's my goal: to go steady with him.

This week I have been praying pretty regular and I think everything I've asked for has come true except for President Kennedy's poor infant son getting better.

Saturday, August 10: I saw Mauri today and I have to admit it was probably unwillingly on his part. Mitch picked me up to go to Hollywood Boulevard with Fran. So on the way to her house he stopped at the parking lot where Mauri works. Mauri looked terrible, he's growing a beard, his hair was real bushy and he broke or did something real bad to the tip of his nose. (He might have to have it redone! Which I think is ridiculous but what does it matter what I think.) It was very awkward talking with him as usual, but even more so today. And I think I'm getting sick, I've been feeling cold all day. We left, picked up Fran and went to Hollywood. On the way home, Mitch got a speeding ticket. I felt so bad and worse because, after they dropped me off, they were going to the beach. I just felt like an ass, like I was imposing and it was my fault that he got a ticket. He wouldn't have been on that street if he didn't have to take me home. I feel like such a heel. Later I called Fran from my babysitting job and she said they ended up at the laundromat, not the beach. Mauri was also there so Mitch asked him if he liked me. He said, "Yes." And if that didn't sound like I asked Fran to tell Mitch to ask him, then I don't know...

Sunday, August 18: Damn Mrs. Sternberg, Harry's mom. She told Mom that when she looked out her dining room window yesterday afternoon, she saw me *with a strange boy* inside Mom's Falcon parked in our driveway. She said she couldn't see our faces, only our legs and feet! Let me explain. A couple of weeks ago I drove to Pico to get Mom something from the Fox Market. I did, but I also went next door to the five and dime and had the car keys duplicated. I didn't tell her. Anyway this was one of those San Ysidro weekends so I decided to "borrow" the car so Fran and I could go to the beach on Saturday. We ended up going to Redondo Beach, which is about 20 miles away. We met the boys there and I drove home with Mauri because he said he could wind back the odometer. I knew exactly what the mileage was before we left. Anyway, that's why we were upside down, feet in the air, in the car. We weren't doing anything like "that." After Mrs. Sternberg told Mom what she saw, Mom checked the car with her "eagle eye" and found a few grains of sand in the back seat and I guess the rest is history…

Monday, September 2: I'm very upset - because of Mauri. Last night I went out with him. We triple dated with Fran and Mitch and another couple. We went to see the play "Come Blow Your Horn," which was good. Mauri was kind of cold to me the first part of the evening. I felt left out. The other two couples are going steady and Mauri wouldn't even hold my hand walking and while we were waiting for the show to start, he wouldn't talk to me. I felt like crying and going away. Hell, he asked me so he might as well have talked to me. I think I talked more with Fran. I was pretty aggravated. Finally when we left, he took my hand. Charge. Then we drove up into the hills, to the empty lot by the "arrow", and parked. We made out for about an hour and a half. Then Mauri was finally friendly. I got upset and confused. Then we left for home and he was cold again just like in the beginning. I felt and still feel like I was being used. At my door I kissed him and told him I had a good time. He didn't answer and that was it. Why did I tell him I had a good time when I know I didn't? What's wrong with me??!

Monday, September 30: School started and I think I'm through with Mauri. I've talked to him once. He told me he thinks he's going to rush the Crusaders (a boys club). I'm still confused about staying in the D'Artagns. Yesterday I went to a swim party at this guy Stan's. It was okay. I can't seem to get interested in anybody else but I'm giving myself only one more week to make something with Mauri and then that's it.

Saturday, October 5: Guy joined the Cub Scouts and today his troop went up to Mount Frazier but we drove Guy up instead of him going with his friends. I don't know why Mom and Dad didn't want him to drive with the group. Anyway, we got up there and couldn't find them and it started snowing! We ended up going to a little log cabin diner and had hot cocoa. Mom was mad but it felt wonderful staring out the foggy window watching the snow fall.

Saturday, November 16: Not much is happening. But I've been thinking over the past year, and I've noticed a lot of things. I think I may be maturing. My opinions have changed about practically everything and everyone but I'm still confused as hell about growing up. It's too hard to figure it all out by yourself. I can't seem to ask Dad about these types of things. He's always unapproachable, physically not there, or sleeping. And I definitely won't be asking Mom. I don't trust her.

Nothing at all ever became of Mauri and me. He got into the Crusaders with Mitch, and Mitch and Fran broke up. That was a shock. Fran and I have sort of drifted apart but…well, we'll see. I talk to Sue more but I'm careful; she's still Sue. I finally had it out with my parents about everything: my small allowance, my curfew that's earlier than everyone else's, having to baby-sit Guy (heck, I was babysitting him when I was younger than he is now) and the way they "are" with me. Why can't they get this about me: I need them to cheer on my big-mouthy side and snuggle and protect my scaredy-cat side. Afterwards things went fairly smoothly, until today – I needed extra money for Sweet Sixteen presents, etc. so I was back in the dog house. Back to square one. But they left for San Ysidro so things cleared themselves up. Thank God for those weekends.

I applied for a job at Silverwood's – hope they call. I'm going to apply tomorrow at May Co. and then go to an employment agency next week. I have got to get a job because my money situation is ridiculous. I would like to start dating again, but not go head-over-heels for any boy. It hurts too much. It's not worth it. But I'd still like to get back into circulation. Andy has written me some postcards from Berkeley. I like him, but he can't be my boyfriend.

Wednesday, November 20: I'm staring out the car window, streaked with rain and listening to the radio on the way to school. Dad has the dial on the news station and JFK just announced that he was saving the life of the Thanksgiving turkey this year and not eating it. That's nice.

Sunday, November 24: I can't believe it – President Kennedy is dead. Friday, the 22nd, he was shot and killed in Dallas Texas at 12:30 p.m.!!! It's so awful, so shocking, so sad.

I was getting dressed in the gym and some girl said, "Kennedy's shot." We all said, "Shut up. Don't be stupid." I walked into my fourth period Physiology class and sat down next to my lab partner, Roger W. The bell rang but Dr. Goldberg wasn't in class yet. He walks in late and you could tell something was wrong. He was weeping; tears were going down his face. Then he spoke and told us what happened. Then the principal got on the PA system and told us again. He also said school was dismissed for the day. I walked home in a daze. All the newspapers had these huge headlines. I'd never seen anything like that.

You have no idea what utter chaos is going on. Dallas officials supposedly found the assassin that very same day and this morning, to top it all off, another man shot the assassin! Guy and I were watching the TV and we saw it happen! How stupid can they be? The assassin's name is Lee Oswald (24 years old) and the man who killed him is Jack Ruby. All the countries around the world are sending their sympathy but also the whole mess must seem so hypocritical to all the other countries. We're supposedly the "land of the free" and all that flag waving stuff. How could something like this happen here? Oh I don't know anymore. I don't understand. It's horrible, you read about bad things in history books but you never think it will ever really happen to you.

Monday, November 25: They buried the president today and I know I will never forget this day, the steady dum-ta-dum of the drums as his body was taken to the church, and then on to the cemetery, will forever ricochet inside me. So heartbreaking, so terrifying.

Saturday, December 14: I feel like I've been in a trance. All I've been doing is watching TV. It's so incredibly depressing and I have this feeling like the floor is falling away under me. Guy watches with me. We're both numb. I don't feel safe. I can't eat.

This afternoon we went shopping with Mom at Fedco and on the way home there was a steady stream of police cars and fire engines that flew past us. I started to panic but Mom kept driving for home. She put on the radio and the announcer said that the Baldwin Hills dam, right up the street from Fedco, had burst! We got home safely, and for the first time since Kennedy was killed we watched something else on TV. We could have been washed away in our car, too. I feel so small and helpless.

I'm staring at the Christmas ads in the newspaper. There's a battery powered JFK doll that sits on a small rocking chair. It plays "Happy Days are Here Again".

Chapter 20:
Love 1964

January: Here's hoping that this year will be happier than last. I feel like I'm nesting, trying to organize my life, my routines. If I am more in charge, maybe, I'll have more chance to not be "surprised" by life. Mom did get me a new bedroom set for my Sweet (?) Sixteen present. It's okay, I guess. Maybe I was getting "too big" for my old bedroom set. I don't know. But it feels like that part of my life is gone. It was the bed I'd slept in since I gave up my crib. This new bedroom set has a smaller twin size bed, a "Hollywood bed," that's pushed into a corner with bolsters so it looks like a small sofa when I'm not sleeping in it. It's modern, with a chest of drawers and matching desk, and it's orange and brown... I forgot to take out the sacred heart pillow that Mommy put in between the mattresses. It's gone.

I'm trying to write more often in French to my cousin Caty. It's easier to write now, but only if I don't write about "feelings". I don't know the "emotional" words too well.

I wrote a letter to the D'Artagns and resigned. I don't regret it or miss them. It just wasn't me.

February: Well I let Mom talk me into a stupid thing: streaking my hair blonde! She said she knew how to do it because of all the time she spent working at Charles of the Ritz. I should have known better. She was only the receptionist there. But I thought it might look good, so she found an old swimming cap, a crochet hook and bought some hair bleach. She poked a bunch of holes in the cap, mixed up the bleach, and pulled the cap over my head. Then she fished out hook-fulls of my hair and pulled it through the cap. I looked like a freak. Dad and Guy, thank God, weren't home. Anyway she painted the bleach on the hair outside of the cap and we waited. She said as dark as my hair is, it bleached out quickly. She washed the bleach out and pulled the cap off. Swear to God, I looked like a zebra! She hadn't pulled the hair tight enough outside of the cap and took way too much hair through each hole. Big chunks of my hair were platinum, except for the first inch closest to my scalp. It looked horrible. By this time it was 7:30 p.m. on a Sunday. Nothing was open, so we ended up at the little drug store in the lobby of the Beverly Wilshire Hotel and bought a bottle of dark brown dye. (I wore a kerchief.) Finally at about 10 p.m. my hair looked fairly normal.

My hair looked okay at school the next day, but every time I wash it, the "stripes" show more and more... I guess I'll have to keep using the brown dye till my hair grows out. What a mess.

I am now a B12! One more year of high school. I have two electives this semester: Senior Yearbook Design and Advanced Sewing. I really enjoy both of them, especially Yearbook. Remember last year that cute guy that I saw on the bus coming home from the beach? Well, he's in the Yearbook class. His name is Jeffrey P. Anyway, it's a small class: fifteen students plus Miss Evans, the teacher. She's great. She talks to us like equals.

I talk more and more with Jeff. We pass notes to each other. Turns out, that he's an A11, half a year behind my class. But he's two weeks older than me. He didn't skip a grade in elementary school like I did. He has a stepfather and doesn't know anything about his real dad. And he's half Jewish. I think I really like him. He is beautiful: he has dirty blond hair, bluish green eyes, and gorgeous teeth. Best of all, he likes to talk about his feelings, how mixed up he feels a lot of the time, and he listens to me. I'm addicted to telling Jeff about my feelings and having it matter to him.

Monday, March 23: Saturday night or Sunday morning, at midnight, Jeff asked me to go steady! He gave me his silver ID bracelet. Now I think I'm the happiest person - inside - in the world. I think I really love him. He's wonderful, I don't exactly know how to put into words what I feel, but it's perfect and beautiful. It's such a feeling of complete contentment to know that someone really cares about me, that I count for someone. Only four people outside of us know. When school starts again after Easter vacation, everyone will know. He has a fan club of girlfriends and he knows just about everyone! I still can't believe he's mine. I wish I could have written down everything he said to me. It was so wonderful. I remember with Mauri I used to feel guilty about things we "did" (not that it was anything to feel guilty about). But that was just it: there was nothing to feel guilty about, but I did anyway.

The first time I went out with Jeff was nine days ago. It was so cute. We went to the movies to see "Dr. Strangelove," and then to Wil Wright's for ice cream. (I saved the little macaroon cookie that comes in a tiny wax paper envelope.) I was worried about what would happen when he dropped me off at home. He kissed me, and that was it. He calls me two or three times a day. I don't know how long that will last. And he comes over about once a day. I call him sometimes too, and the most special thing is that I can talk to him, really talk, like a real friend.

April: I had to see a counselor at school because I haven't been clear about my "college preparatory classes." He asked me lots of questions about what I'm interested in and my goals and as usual I didn't know and I couldn't explain myself. Sometimes when I feel I'm being cornered or put on the spot my mind goes blank and I can't think. I just want to shrink back like a snail. Anyway he gave me a very long aptitude test. Guess what? I scored 99 percent in Mechanical Arts! So I suppose that means I should become a mechanic. But you know what, I am doing very well in my Advanced Sewing class and I do use a "machine". The class is great except for one thing: not having enough money for the fabric I need. Mom says if I can't find what I want at Newberry's that's too bad. But Gail, Jeff's friend and neighbor, is in this class too and realizes she hates to sew. Her mom bought her this gorgeous tweed wool for a lined coat Gail's supposed to be making. She asked if I could make it for her and I could use it as my final project as long as she gets the coat to show her mom! Deal.

On weekends Jeff and I go surfing; well, he goes surfing and I watch. He picks me up very early in the morning before the sun rises. His stepfather repossesses cars so Jeff usually has a car he can "borrow." I sneak out my window and get back before anyone notices I'm gone.

Saturday, May 8: Jeff doesn't want to go steady anymore but he says I can keep his ID bracelet. I don't exactly know why – I can't understand it but it feels like we are still going steady. It's not as if life is anew again, so unbelievably good, but just that I think I have a new outlook on it. I have so many more friends now, it's, well, unbelievable. Both girls and boys. Only yesterday a guy off the street went to all the trouble to call this girl I had recently met for my phone number! I walk differently; I have a goofy smile on my face and sing to myself. Jeff still calls two or three times a day. Between classes we hide in the shadows under the stairs and sneak a kiss or two. I wish I could see the future about Jeff and me, school, everything. Well, maybe not. Funny if it turns out that I marry him. But, on second thought, I'm not so hip on the idea anymore. I don't want to be tied down as of yet, not for at least five to eight years. I don't know. The issue of having kids is the real problem and being a mom.

Wednesday, June 10: The family, including me, is supposed to go to New York for five days. It sounds exciting, but I don't know if I really want to go. To be frank, I'd be wondering about Jeff so far away, and second of all I'm scared stiff of going on a jet. Sounds ridiculous, I know, but I'm scared. I keep telling myself if it's my time to die, then I'll die – it's already written in the book of life. But when it comes to applying my philosophy, the scene changes. I have to make up my mind soon. I'm not sure when they want to go but I think it's around the time of the Shoe Trade Show, whenever that is.

Friday, July 10: Well, they went and I didn't. Since they came back it's been nothing but fights. I need to move out. Either that or I'll have to run away. Obviously everyone agrees. Mom and Dad and I, agree that without my presence things would be better all around. I don't think that a 17 year old girl should have to be as miserable and unhappy as I am. I don't mean in a material sense – I know I have more than most girls my age. For a long time I actually believed that the way I felt was all of my own doing. But as time went by, things got progressively worse. First it was Mom only, but now it even includes Dad. Dad has become both unreasonable and impossible to please. He wants me to keep Mom happy, doing, probably anticipate doing, everything that she wants. I can't read her mind. And anyway, why is it my job to keep her happy? I bet he just wants her to stop complaining to him about me. I'm sure his intentions are for the best, but his ideas never seem to work out that way. Nothing I say or do pleases my parents. They don't like most of my friends. This is not what a family should be like. I feel that there is no real communication or human feeling between anyone in the family – it's just a bunch of phoniness, even at the best of times. I also believe that there is nothing either of them or I can do to help this situation. I know that I have tried everything. I am not running away from the problem, but at the same time I do not want to become a nervous wreck by the age of 18! Dad told me once that for his sake I should try to be "good," even if it kills me just to make his last years "happier." (!) Well I can honestly say I've withstood everything I can. I think Mom brings about the "misery," as she calls it, herself by provoking it and Dad intensifies it when he usually doesn't have a clue what the situation happens to be about. Mom seems to look for trouble. I most certainly don't try and bring it on myself. But there's a limit to how much a person can take without "blowing up." What they consider my "blowing up" is nothing compared to what I really feel inside!

Neither of them has tried to understand me or anyone else, for that matter. I am, regardless what they may think, a product of the people and experiences around me. And if they don't like what they see in me, that's how they brought me up. I know that I cannot legally leave without their consent and I know that there is only one place where I could possible live: with my great aunt. God I am so desperate if I'm even considering this. I have written her a letter vaguely describing the situation and what my plans are, but I haven't sent it yet. Now I have to find a way to talk to Dad alone. This problem isn't going away.

Saturday, August 1: Well I am obviously still living at home. I didn't send Aunt Pauline the letter. I tried to talk to Dad, but he won't listen to me. And I get too upset to make any sense. I always start crying. Damn. A couple of days ago I wrote him a letter, mailed it to the factory address. Less chance Mom will know about it. Anyway, I changed tactics. I asked if it would be a "possibility to get a car in the future"; asked how much it would cost for insurance, down payment and upkeep. I explained that as I would be starting college next February, I would really need a car and since I wouldn't be going to a university, my tuition would be much less. I reminded him that he had promised me his old car for my 17th birthday. My birthday came and went, and no car. He did buy a new car for himself, but I haven't been allowed to use it and he traded in his old car instead of giving it to me. He told me that I'd have a car to use within two months after my birthday. Well it's been three months and still no car. I told him I'd be willing to use my own money. I have my Home Savings bank account and all the savings bonds that Kanka gave me. I think that I could pay off the car with my own money over time, but he's keeping me in the dark about everything. Even if he's changed his mind about getting me a car, I wish he would just give me an answer.

Sunday, August 9: Jesus! Dad, Mom and Guy's car was hit by a man who fell asleep while he was driving. The trunk of the new Galaxie is gone! Sheared off!! Thank God they're all right. Guy was sitting in the back seat and now he has to wear a neck brace. They were coming back from one of the San Ysidro weekend trips.

Jeff and I were together today and into the night. He sort of moved out of his house. He's now living in the little apartment that sits on top of their garage. He can play his drums and his parents don't hear it anymore, but best of all we can be alone without his parents or little brothers bothering us. Tonight we were going up the stairs to his apartment and when we got to the top before he opened the door we hugged and kissed. Then it started feeling different, sort of desperate, frantic for both of us, I think. I've never really felt this way before. We were touching each other so intensely, rubbing up against each other that I felt so good, so excited. I know Jeff did too. He opened the door and we sort of fell into his room and on his bed. It was dark and we took each other's clothes off. We kept hugging each other and kissing, feeling the warmth of one another's bodies. I touched his penis and he touched me too, between my legs. He touched my breasts. I started pushing up against him with my vagina so hard that I felt I was flying, falling – it was so wonderful. We were both breathing so hard. He didn't put his penis inside me but I wanted him to. I rubbed his penis so much that white creamy stuff came out in my hand. He was so wound-up, he kept saying my name and God's name. Oh I want to do this again. I love Jeff so much.

September: I am now an A12, my last semester at Fairfax. I am so ready to graduate – I'm tired of high school but at the same time I'm still not sure about what I'm going to do afterwards. I didn't have the right classes to get into UCLA, so I'll be going to Valley State. I am not motivated and I still haven't declared a major.

I did become friendly with some other girls in my class: Linda, Patty and Joyce. None of them are in clubs, which is a good thing. I still love Jeff but I sort of like this guy Roger W. He's really cute and sweet. He was my science lab partner last year. We might go on a hayride in a couple of weeks. I'm going with Linda soon to see "A Hard Day's Night" for the third time at the Pan Pacific Theater. I love the Beatles.

Jeff and I have been going to these "happenings." They're a kind of weird art experience. The first one was at a vacant lot on Pico Boulevard during the day. Someone had brought tons of ice blocks and started building a kind of a structure with them. We stood around and watched it melt. Strange. The other "happening" was in this house in West Hollywood. This one was kind of scary. The inside of the house was empty except for this old grand piano. We were all standing around, and then someone brought in these buckets of pig's blood and boxes full of little live white mice. Then they started pouring the blood all over the piano and the floor and turned over the boxes of mice. Someone started chopping up the piano. Jeff and I were horrified and we started trying to collect all the mice that were running all over. We left. It was awful. That's not art.

October: I cried in Yearbook class today – again. This time Miss Evans sent me to the Girls' Vice-Principal. I guess because I have pretty good grades she paid attention to what I had to say. The GVP wanted to know why I was crying in class and I explained that I have problems at home. She made a call, then gave me a pass, and directed me to go across the street to the Jewish Women's Welfare Organization. Long story short, I sat and talked to a young woman who listened to me talk about my family. She asked if I thought they, Mom and Dad, would come to a meeting with her. I said I wasn't sure. She asked me to ask them. Oh boy. Anyway, I went home and during dinner I asked. Dad was furious. I think he was embarrassed.

But in the end they came to the meeting the next week. It was incredibly uncomfortable. Guy came too. And to make matters worse, Dad got into a car accident in the Canter's Deli parking lot next door. The next meeting I had with the counselor (I think she's an apprentice to being a psychologist, I'm not sure) she advised that as soon as I'm able I should move away from home. (!!) It made me feel a little like when I talk to Dr. Z or Evelyn. I don't feel crazy and bad. Some adults can understand and care about what I experience and feel.

November: I started pulling off my braces myself. I know that they're not done yet with my teeth, but I am done with them. My teeth look good enough and I want to take my senior pictures without braces on my teeth. It's been nearly four years.

Friday, December 11: I got a postcard from Andy today. He's still up at Berkeley. And I'm grounded again. I just heard the phone ring. It's Jeff. Dad answered. He didn't even tell me that Jeff called. I hate them so much. I wish Jeff had told him where to go.

Sunday, December 27: I'm on "vacation" in Arizona with the family. Let's see, to catch up: I'm friends with Patty now. She lives with her dad in an apartment. Her mom is in a mental institution. I ran away from home twice to Patty's. The last time, Dad figured out where I was and threatened to call the police and have Patty's dad arrested for "contributing to the delinquency of a minor". Patty's dad was sympathetic but said he couldn't continue to host me. I went home. Basically I've been grounded ever since, no allowance, etc. I'm still dating Jeff. It's been nearly 10 months. I never really thought we'd make it this far, but we have. I believe I love him and he feels exactly the same. We have made plans for college together and marriage in perhaps four years. He has lots of growing up to do, in areas which I think I have already matured. He does have a better attitude about many things than I do, though. I still make problems for myself out of nothing. Always worrying. Most of my friends don't seem to worry like I do. I have become a great friend to lots of boys. I, in fact, "picked up" a real cute guy named Johnny B. at Delores' Drive-in on "cruise" night last month. We had a real good time, making out on Patty's couch. I never went out with him again, but we're still friends. Things are the same with Mom and Dad. I don't think I'll ever completely get along with them. But I am good friends with both of my brothers, although my relationship with Andy will never be quite normal. I believe he's having a hard time finding a good girlfriend, somebody to help straighten him out. He's 21 years old now and he's about as stable as I am, which isn't saying much. Well, "Mother" just told me to shut up.

Chapter 21:
Clutch 1965

Friday, January 1: I'm still in Phoenix, Arizona with the family. Last night I watched a one-man band at the hotel nightclub. It wasn't bad. He played everything terrifically, and was drunk on top of it! I'd never seen so many crazy adults in one place at the same time. One lady was wearing a dress that lit up like a Christmas tree complete with different colored lights. In spite of everything, it's actually been fun in Arizona. I love the nights. It's so dark here that you can actually see millions of stars twinkling. It's magical.

In exactly 27 days I'll be graduating from high school. And it will be 133 days until Jeff graduates. Caty wrote from France that she wants me to come next summer, the summer of 1966, so we can travel together all over Europe. I'll be 18 this year so it might be easier for me to get a real job. I need to work.

We didn't go to prom, Jeff didn't want to but we got dressed up anyways and went out to Truman's Drive-in restaurant in Westwood Village. He managed to spill his chocolate malted all over my long gown – which I made by the way.

Thursday, January 28: Tonight I graduated! I wore a white cap and gown. Dad, Mom, Guy and Jeff came. After I received my diploma, I walked down the aisle of the auditorium to the strains of "Pomp and Circumstance" and Jeff rushed up and grabbed me around my waist, picked me up and kissed me. He told me how proud he was of me. I felt so special.

I start Valley State College in three weeks. My classes will be: Psychology 101, Sociology 101, Western History and English 101. I am tentatively a Psychology major. And today Dad took me to Frank Taylor Ford to buy me a six-cylinder, stick shift, orange Mustang! I told Dad I wanted a stick shift. My reasons, which I didn't explain to him, were because that's what race cars have and all the guys have stick shift cars. While Dad and the salesman were standing in front of the car I decided to start it up. The car lurched forward. Dad and the salesman jumped. I didn't know Dad could move so fast. I was so embarrassed and horrified. Dad drove the Mustang home and I drove his car. (It's an automatic.)

Well, I've got to learn how to drive this car and I have less than three weeks to do it. First of all, I have to remember to put the clutch down when I start the engine. I've been backing down the driveway and then driving forward all day. Haven't lurched or stalled but it's not the same as driving on a freeway. Valley State is about 18 miles one way! My friend Linda suggested driving to her house and she'd sit with me for moral support while I practice. She lives two miles away. Oh boy.

Well, all the gardeners working on Linda's street today must think I'm nuts. We have lurched, bucked and stalled a hundred times while circling the block but I think it's beginning to sink in. It feels almost like patting your head and rubbing your belly at the same time, trying to shift gears, press the clutch, watch where you're going and use the gas and brake pedals correctly. Linda was so patient. And brave.

Sunday, March 14: Today, rather tonight (it's only 12:30 a.m.) is sort of a milestone for me. I am still with Jeff. It's been exactly one year. One whole year. At times I feel it was a waste and at other times it feels like it's been the greatest year of my life. This past year I feel that I have come to know myself better. I've watched myself handle situations, sometimes failing and other times succeeding. I can't believe it but I think I'm growing up underneath my little girl shell. "The Future" is getting close, so close that time seems to fly. I wonder all the time, "Am I sure about Jeff?" "Is he the one?" because I guess I feel, well not exactly superior, but like I am able to watch the both of us from a distance and seeing the whole, real picture. No matter what else is important to me now and in the future it will and must involve someone else to help me live life. I want to know, to be sure, but I guess that's the way life is: full of guesses and mysteries. Superficially (or materially) I got my "fast" car. Since graduation and starting college I feel I am running around in circles. I don't know what the hell I'm doing in college. But like a blind man, I keep fumbling.

I think the year with Jeff was more than a milestone in one sense: I actually remained best friends with him. We confide everything to each other, but I still always get hurt by him. To be honest, I'm hurting right now. He stood me up - again. But tonight or in another day it will become quite irrelevant. But I continue to have that "I could kick myself in the pants" feeling. I've dated about six other guys this year, but Jeff has become a habit I can't break. I give up too many things because I guess I won't let myself have fun with anyone else. It's always him that's on my mind – always! He's almost my obsession. Love has become the most indefinable word for me except that "Jeff" = "happiness" = "love" to me. He is the first boy that covered all my requirements. He helped me to grow up without realizing it. People respect me, maybe envy me. That's what makes it so weird when I absolutely fall apart if grubby, messy ole Jeff doesn't call or say "hello" the way I'd like to hear it. Funny? Maybe. But the funniness could float in the tears I've cried sometimes. Worth it? Yes, yes, yes. I have to believe its "yes." I've made it be "yes." We communicate. It's the first time in my life that I've ever really felt listened to. But that's my problem: obviously I'm not independent, and part of me needs that independence. I'll never be able to do anything successfully unless I try. Onward!

April: Valley State is not what I expected. It feels like high school just with more space and lots of orange trees. And I don't like driving here. I'm very good at shifting gears now, but I've had some scary experiences. While on the freeway, I hit two dogs that were mating in the fast lane. It was awful. I shake every time I think about it. When it rains, all the surface streets flood. I lost my brakes driving as I entered the submerged school parking lot. I had to keep circling for about 15 minutes until the car slowed down. And today some other student hit my car near the college. I recognized him. He's the crippled son of one of Dad's business associates. I didn't say anything. My grill was damaged, the chrome mustang fell off. As soon as this semester ends, I think I'm going to transfer to Los Angeles City College (LACC). Most everyone from Fairfax is there.

Tuesday, April 13: I am so furious. I walked in the house today and something caught my eye as I was closing the front door: a new spinet piano! I walked into the living room and turned toward the front window and my baby grand piano was gone!! I ran to find Mom and asked what happened and she told me she traded *my* piano in for this new one. Why? Because it matches the new living room furniture better!! I howled, yelled, cried. How dare she do that without asking me first? I called Dad at work and he had nothing to say. I am so upset. I hate them.

June: Well, I got my grades in the mail today: three C's and one D and I'm officially on probation. The D is in Psychology, my declared major! I have never done so badly in school. And I have to take an entrance exam in order to transfer to LACC.

My friend Linda is making me feel uncomfortable. Sometimes I feel like I'm walking on eggs when I'm with her. She's kind of moody, and it's hard for me to tell how she's feeling. I feel like I'm obligated to call her or go out with her. It doesn't feel natural. We had a talk and hopefully that will help things. I told her that I thought she acts unhappy some of the time. I tried to explain that I have lots of friends and don't just hang out with one. I hope she's not disappointed. She says she's not. It feels a little suffocating for me.

Monday, June 21: I got a job!! I am working part-time at the Sears and Roebuck Credit Department. My hours are 5:30 – 9:30 PM Monday through Friday and I'm getting paid $1.75 an hour. The work is kind of boring. I don't work with the customers but downstairs in the basement. My job is to open payment envelopes and separate the payment from the statement, making sure the amounts match. Most people send checks, but some send cash or postage stamps. Sometimes the envelope is from someone famous, like Cary Grant, and I can save the envelopes with the cancelled stamps for myself. But it's a real job. I make about $35 a week!

Friday, August 13: Tonight when I was at work my boss told me and the two other girls to get up quickly and follow him. We went down a hallway and he unlocked a door that led into the Wilshire Division Police Department that's next door. He said we needed to wait until it was safe for us to leave and go home. Two days ago some Negroes started rioting in Watts. Tonight they've been looting and burning stores, and it's getting close to where we are. I was able to go home at about 7 p.m. Harry from next door came over and said his dad's grocery/liquor store was burnt down on Central Avenue!! I don't understand what's going on. Dad didn't say anything.

September: I took the LACC entrance exam and got a postcard telling me I could enroll, and to see a counselor because I got 100 percent (!) on the exam. I am now, tentatively, an Accounting major. I will be taking another history class, Bookkeeping, Gym (you still have to take a gym class in junior college), and Philosophy. I'm more comfortable here, there are more familiar faces, and I like the way the school looks. I guess I just love old-fashioned buildings. I haven't met with a counselor yet, though. I'm carpooling with Rachel. It's so good to be seeing her on an everyday basis again. I like her. She's very steady, not too emotional or clingy. I just wish her parents would like me better. I can't help it if I'm half Jewish. Rachel is sneaking out with Brian Doyle. He's definitely not even half Jewish.

I'm having terrible belly aches, cramps some days. I am continuously reading more into situations and things people say to me than I know I should. Jeff says that I love to make myself suffer. I wonder. Yes, we're still together but I feel starved for affection. Physical affection would probably temporarily satiate me. As always, my parents, especially Mom, are driving me crazy. I guess because she can't get her hands on my paycheck and Andy's not around she has to ratchet things up and find new ways to torture me. I hate her and hate Dad for not rescuing me.

I met a beautiful girl at work. Our boss brought her down to introduce her to our "team." She looks like an angel. Honestly, she has natural blonde hair, blue eyes, a tiny nose and the most beguiling smile. Her name is Dori. She's an English Literature major at UCLA. She's very nice, with a soft voice. I think she's a couple of years older than me.

I was trained to use a 10-key adding machine last week, and I'm pretty fast. The girls on our team sort of compete. It's not so boring now. Tonight Dori asked me if she could tell me the story of "Othello" by William Shakespeare while we work. She says it will help her study for her exam. I've only read "Julius Caesar" and "Romeo and Juliet" so I said "Yes!" Work just flew by, she made the story so interesting! We've exchanged phone numbers and made tentative plans to go ice skating at the Polar Palace in Hollywood.

October: Mark, one of Jeff's friends, killed an old woman crossing Sixth Street!! He was driving at night and didn't see her and his car knocked her down. It's awful. I still shake when I think of those dogs I hit. I can't imagine how he feels. He lost his license. And Jeff borrowed my car and got into an accident. He smashed in the front and cracked the radiator. But no one got hurt. I made up a story why I needed to sleep over at Linda's house for the three days it took to fix the car. I had to loan Jeff the $250 to fix it. I withdrew the money from my savings account. When I returned home, I caught Dad looking at my car and opening the hood. I think he knows what happened because later, when I lifted the hood to look, I saw there was still a circular mark etched on the back of the radiator. Jeff paid me back.

November: I had a weird and scary experience with Jeff tonight. He found out about this group of people that's trying to help Negroes get jobs, so he asked me to go to one of their meetings. The place, actually an empty warehouse, was on Central Avenue and 42nd Street near where Harold's Dad's liquor store used to be. We parked and went in. Mike and I were the only white people there, which was okay but I got really nervous when I saw all these rifles propped up against one of the walls. The group is called Operation Bootstrap but I couldn't pay attention to what anyone was saying except those guns. I don't think I'm going to go back even if Jeff decides to.

I finally wrote Harriet, it's been months. I'm kind of depressed, feeling lost. My parents are acting the same. I'm so uncomfortable in my own home. I feel bad about Guy but I think he's actually doing okay with both of them. He's so much younger than me. I have nothing in common with him. I still have Mitou and Evelyn. That's so sad that the only two beings in my own home that I can confide in are my cat and the housekeeper but I am grateful. I'm still not inspired by school and I'll have to probably change my major again. I'm doing lousy in Bookkeeping. I've had three major fights with Jeff in the past six months. I kept trying to change him, reform him and I'm the only one who came out different: sadder and wiser. It really was a mature and sincere relationship while it lasted, but it's ending up being me "giving" and "getting" little in return. I know he's seeing other people, so am I, but I love him. I'm thinking I love him, but maybe I don't know what love is.

I became friendly with one of Jeff's girlfriends, a neighbor. Janice is also the on-and-off girlfriend of his best friend Mark. I knew Mark before I met her. And because I knew things she would have liked to know and vice versa, we became friends. Unfortunately in early September Mark and I became enemies. He said I was talking behind his back. Then he killed that old lady. After that we became friends again, just not as close. So the four of us - Mark, Janice, Jeff and myself - became intertwined friends. And we talked a lot in different paired groups at different times. It felt like a game of "telephone", the truth always garbled and many times "something" was made out of absolutely nothing. While all this was going on I had no time for my old girl friends. We gradually lost touch. All of us go to LACC except Janice, who's still at Fairfax.

Saturday, December 25: Merry Christmas. All I want for Christmas is…a steady boyfriend. I need this for the security it brings, because of knowing there's someone who'll always be waiting for me, thinking of me first, someone to identify with. Not someone to compete with! Jeff and I are really not seeing each other anymore: no dates, no nothing. I realized if I didn't drive over to his house/apartment, assuming he'd even be there, we wouldn't have any contact. I'm tired of being the "pursuer." Finally last week, I heard through the grapevine that he wanted to break up. I realized it wasn't the end of the world, and I could go on without him and find someone else. I was happy, real happy. Then he called. Jeff confused me when he said he wanted me. Not all of me but just enough to "recharge" himself, so he could go on with everything else. At least he was honest about that. But it left me so confused. A boy that I honestly loved for almost two years breaks up with me, then comes back. When he called I debated whether to tell him not to call me again but I couldn't. He told me he feels confused, I understand 'confused,' but this is something the two of us have to sort out alone, ourselves, without "advice" from everyone else. Jeff says he feels tied down by our relationship. I don't want that. I feel so sad.

Chapter 22:
My Turn 1966

Saturday, January 1: I got one really good Christmas present: the family spent the last week in Las Vegas without me. They just got home. Now for my resolutions: try to be as honest as possible, especially with myself; have a good boy-girl relationship; get serious about school; have a mind of my own; save my money; get Friday nights off; not gossip so much and not worry about everything!!!

Tuesday, January 4: Talked to Jeff's mom today and she told me she'd like me as a daughter-in-law (!!!), but that her son is too confused and immature. Where did that come from?! He calls once or twice a week and I, unfortunately, drive by his house almost every day. I have to stop doing that.

Wednesday, January 5: I got Fridays off! But now I work all day on Saturdays. I'm being trained to be an encoder on one of their big Burroughs encoding machines. The credit department has two encoders and two card keypunchers. If I'm good enough, I can get a raise! Dori and I are going horseback riding at Pickwick Stables. We've gone twice already. I really enjoy her company.

Friday, January 7: I did exactly what I said I wouldn't: I stopped at Jeff's and it didn't go well. Then to make matters worse, I called him from school. He said he only wanted to be friends. I felt hurt and mad. Then he asked if I wanted to go for a quick dinner with him, and like a jerk I said "Yes". We ate and then he went home to paint his room. Now everything seems okay until the next time. Jeez, I'm going to be 19 years old this year. When am I going to grow up?

I'm lying here on my Hollywood bed, staring at the ceiling, and I hear tapping at my window. I get up and he's standing there. It's almost 10 p.m. I lift the window sash and he asks why I didn't come back or call.

This is what's so hard: what does he want from me? I love him so much it hurts. I lean out the window and we hold on to each other for dear life.

I keep driving by Jeff's. I have to stop this. I'm always wondering what he's doing. I feel so mixed up inside but somehow I can't break this off.

Wednesday, January 19: Jeff came to school but he had no classes. He said he was waiting for me. I was suspicious, but he didn't seem to notice. We traded car keys, and he drove my car and I drove his T-Bird to the Farmer's Market to visit his mom and grandma. (They run a fruit and vegetable stand.) Later Janice called me and told me he made a date with "Pam." I'm glad. It's a shame he couldn't tell me, but after all I had it coming. He told Janice that he still liked me. Charge. I'm not upset. Really.

Mother is acting up again. She's nuts, I'm sure of it. I think she's jealous of me, maybe because of Dad. But that makes no sense because I have virtually no relationship with him anymore if ever. I can't figure out any other reason. It's not my job to make her "better". I'm the one suffering. I get upset, literally sick to my stomach. I am the same person at home as I am elsewhere. But according to her I'm too moody, a slob, I don't eat right etc. etc. Sometimes she's a doll and other times, like today, she's a witch. Some of the things she used to complain about had some basis but now they don't. For example, knock before entering her bedroom (Dad's not even home) even though the lights and TV are on, but she can walk in on me without knocking when I'm sitting on the toilet. I don't care, but I did make the mistake of mentioning it and she said, "I make the rules and if you don't like it, get out!" That seems like the only solution, but I can't afford it and I won't ask Dad for the money. So?? My friends have fights with their parents too, but this is different. My friends know they're loved, that they matter.

Thursday, January 20: What a day. First I had my finals, and considering I didn't really study, it will be a miracle if I pass any of my classes. Anyway, I left school and came home early. As soon as I walked in Mother told me to call "your father." She was not happy. I called Dad at work. He came on the phone and his voice sounded so stern, all business. He said, "Do you want me to divorce your mother? Well, I will not. You need to move out. I will pay you $85 a month for an apartment. You have three weeks to find one." I didn't say anything except "Okay." I know it is for the best. I feel numb and excited. Does that makes sense?

As usual there was no conversation when Dad came home. Mom seems smug or relieved. Who knows and who cares. I think Dad feels relieved too, but guilty, at the same time. He should have defended me.

Now for my hair, today I bleached my whole head! First it was so light and red but then I went to Janice's and we put on "Moonhaze" and "Starlight". It's very pretty now. We'll see if blondes really do have more fun!

I didn't go to work and I'm off tomorrow. Jeff called but I wouldn't talk to him. I am going out of my mind about it though.

Friday, January 21: Today was, by far, the worst day. First I went to school, then home and then to Linda's to help her do her hair. I went back home and Janice called to tell me that Jeff did ask Pam out and probably will again next week. Then she said that Jeff is going out with Linda (!) this Saturday night. I was so upset and shocked. I was just with Linda. She didn't say a word. I asked Janice if she could go out but she couldn't so I called Simone. I needed to talk to someone. Simone said she could meet me for coffee at 8:15. Just as I was leaving, the phone rang and it was Jeff. I was terribly cold to him. He asked if we could talk. I said if I had time I would stop by. After I left Simone, I stopped at Jeff's. I pulled into the driveway and honked. He came down and got into the passenger seat. We started to talk but he didn't say anything about Pam. Here I'm stuck knowing about Pam (and Linda) and supposed to not know, and he's not saying anything about it! Then I mentioned that I was moving out of my parents' house. He asked, "Aren't we close enough that you could have told me before?" I was so upset, I didn't know what to say. But finally I told him that after I move out, it would be a new semester and I will be starting fresh and that we'd better not see each other for a while.

Jeff opened the car door and started out, saying, "I thought you loved me." I said I had loved him and do love him and probably will love him for some time, but I didn't want to take any more shit from him.

Sunday, January 23: I called Linda and asked her to tell me what happened when she went out with Jeff. She was a bit shocked but said "Okay". She said that she and her friend Jacki went out with Jeff and saw a movie, "The Loved One." She asked if I was mad. Ha! I don't even remember what I said.

I wrote a letter to Jeff, but this time I'm going to hold on to it for a while. It was good to put everything down on paper, though. It helped clarify things a bit. We are both so immature. And all the conversations that fly around between Janice, Mark, Linda, Jeff and me make everything into something it's not. It's gossip, really. The main problems stem from Mark and Janice. It shouldn't involve them. They seem to know more stuff than anyone else. How can that be right?

But, jeez, who am I kidding? I have hardly any self-respect. Jeff deliberately hid the truth from me and tried to turn the situation around and make me the bad guy. I believed I loved him, but I also remember the first time he "let me down easy," saying that he didn't want to feel obligated to me - that he hated that feeling. That's why he despises authority, his job, school, his parents, and me. But unfortunately he needed me. I was the first person that ever took the time to understand him. I can't change him. But I can change myself.

Tuesday, January 25: Andy's home. I guess he's done at Berkeley. I've been looking at apartments, but nothing yet. Andy and I went to lunch and had a good talk. I told him about what happened with 'Mother' and 'Father.' I also told him I'm thinking about transferring to San Francisco State. It would be good to get away. He seemed a little lost.

Monday, January 30: I found an apartment! It's a furnished single with utilities included. The rent will be $85 a month, just what Dad's willing to pay. I move in on <u>Tuesday, February 8</u>! It's in West Hollywood, one block east of La Cienega Boulevard, near Melrose Avenue. The only problem might be parking, especially on Mondays, Art Gallery night. It's street parking only, no garage.

This will be good.

Monday, February 7: I am packing up my stuff: clothes, books, records etc. I decided to tell Mom that I'm taking the spinet piano. She said absolutely not. She doesn't even play the piano. Dad said nothing. It was worth a shot though.

Tuesday, February 8: Parting was on the best of terms: Mom actually let me make my own tuna sandwich yesterday. And I've even been invited to join them for dinner when they go out on Fridays. We might be able to talk to each other. Anything is possible.

Wednesday, February 9: I open my eyes and scan the ceiling. I can't believe it – I am waking up in my own apartment. Here I am, lying in a strange bed, alone in this nice, little courtyard apartment. It's a bit musty and old but most important, it's mine!! I finally have my own phone, and wander around freely, open cupboards, drawers and just be me. No 'sound track' of Mom's non-verbal noises of disapproval. Wonderful sweet silence. I'm going to be okay. No I am already okay.

I don't need to keep trying to get attention and love from my parents or anyone. I'll start with loving me. I am going to make it.

And who knows, maybe now I can fill the silences with the echoes of the words and breath that prove my mom, my real mom, existed and loved me.

Epilogue

Does everyone count things? I always seem to be counting things, double checking, inventorying. Today I counted that nearly 85 hairs fell out of my head after I washed, dried and brushed my hair; that there were only two bees among the lavender. Counting how many days, months, years my mom was alive, how many I've been alive. Counting.

I finished reading the red 'Daily Reminders' that my mother wrote in French. Her last, for 1957, the year she died. I had scanned them before, but didn't actually read them. I evidently wasn't ready to "hear" the words in the diaries then, and now I'm not sure I like the picture of my mother that's being revealed. Part of me knows that because she was probably already sick in 1950 when I was only three, it would be unfair to characterize her by her words so many years later. I can now understand after becoming a mother, how my words, actions or inactions might have affected my own children. Even though I was not ill, I remember being so preoccupied by my own personal issues that my children did not always get the best of me. I wouldn't want my journals taken too literally all these years later.

My mother was definitely physically uncomfortable in 1955 and 1956, and certainly in unbearable pain near the end. The many physicians she saw during the last five years of her life only treated her symptoms and not the disease itself, and probably perceived her as an emotional woman who needed drugs "to settle her nerves."

But there's still something else, her impatience with people (but, interestingly, not my dad), her restlessness and most painful to read about was her apparent annoyance at having to deal with her children. Perhaps being the firstborn and a reasonably "easy" baby and toddler, I got the best of her mothering. I'll never know for sure. However because one of the rare times I actually asked my dad a question about their relationship straight out, why there was such an age gap between me and my brother, I did learn this: I was supposed to be an only child. But because my mother was already having "female difficulties," a doctor thought that going through another pregnancy might "regulate her system." Guy was born. He was not an easy child. He was sick a lot, and wouldn't eat much. He wasn't thriving, not even growing as expected. Mom didn't write too much about us. But when she did, she complained about him. After the fourth entry stating that Guy had wandered off again, I wondered how involved she really was with us as her children, and how much attention she paid. It seemed that our basic needs were taken care of, but otherwise our mother really couldn't be bothered with my brother or me. We annoyed her: that is what I first understood when I read her diaries but today I understand it differently. She didn't choose to ignore us – her disease was taking all her focus. She was too distracted by her pain to pay much attention to her children. She couldn't be guilty of all the good she could have done. Her written words were of a specific moment in time.

The last entries were written by my father in English. It was heart breaking. He carefully detailed all of her medical treatments, promises made by doctors, her state of mind and the unbearable suffering she went through. He wrote fifty-nine journal entries. His last, "My poor Nisou expired at 11:45 am. My story – the happiest episode of my life came to an end. Rest in peace, my darling! Rest in peace!" Inserted with the last entry were the receipts for the cemetery plot and the granite marker for her grave.

My dad's silent instruction was that my mother was not to be spoken of, revered, but without mention. She was like our little secret. But I needed him to talk about his feelings, model for me what to do. I ached for longing itself, the state of pure hope that young children have and then as adults are nostalgic for, for the rest of their lives. At first when my mother died, my grief was numbing, then it buried itself like a tiny splinter I didn't even realize I had until it festered so deep it had nowhere to go but in my heart. I knew I was hurting but I didn't know why.

Dad emotionally vanished and then came back as someone else with a new wife, our new mom.

I was so torn, just a young girl of 12 who would have been normally moving emotionally away from my father but there was no mother there to pick up the slack. My stepmother was emotionally unavailable. And I only had fleeting female role models. Womanhood was looking scary and hard. So I guess I coped by burying all my memories of my mom and lashing out at my parents. They never seemed to include me, approve of me or show me any affection. I needed to be parented, nurtured, and supported. I didn't know how to ask for it and kept waiting and hoping for it to happen. It never did.

After I moved away from home, I finally had the emotional space to remember my mother. The stress was gone from living with my parents. I could breathe and stop worrying about what might upset my stepmother next. I resigned as guardian of her moods. I had failed in that role anyway. I found addresses of my mother's old friends, her relatives. When I was 19, I wrote to them, "reintroducing" myself, asking for stories, anything that would help capture her essence for me. Most wrote back. It was wonderful. I was beginning to fill in the blanks. Now I knew I had to engage in her things, her diaries, books, and letters. I needed to know what part of her was in me. Would she have approved of my life? My choices? Would we have been friends? I finally cried. I sobbed and I mourned for all that was lost.

I never gave up hoping Dad would volunteer some memories, stories about their past, but wistful looks were all he was able to give me. When he died, those possibilities ended. However, I didn't know he had saved everything of their life together, boxed up in the garage. Perhaps that's where he hid his pain.

My stepmother, who threw out and changed so many things, didn't touch those items, thank God. But I had to wait until I was 54 years old to discover them. The day after my stepmother died, I learned while reading her will that she had been married three times before she met my father and had never married my stepbrother's father. Her own father died in Auschwitz. No other information, no background. I was left to wonder how this had affected her and colored her future relationships.

So it seems that my parents, all my parents: my real mother, my father and my stepmother loved and cared for me the best they could at the time. I know my dad loved me, but he couldn't express it. I understand that my stepmother had emotional baggage that had nothing to do with me. And my mother was a strong woman who left her homeland with a man she loved and they had a child that they cherished and probably spoiled. And then my mother became very ill and died.

For a long time the memory of my mother had been replaced by static photos, frozen in my mind. She didn't move: her gestures, tone of voice were lost to me. But while researching for this book I found a photo taken of her (by my future father), laying asleep in the grass with her arms outstretched over her head. Suddenly I had a 'muscle memory.' An echo of that gesture lives in me. It's as if her hand had reached out and taken mine.

Hidden in their garage I find some linen napkins, each one monogrammed with the letter H. They belonged to my mother's French family. I gingerly unfold them. Taking a pencil to paper, I sketch each step as I unfold until I am sure I can refold them exactly as they were. I pretend I can still feel the warmth of my mother's hands on them. It's almost like trying to catch a bubble, remembering a scent, saving it for good.

www.ingramcontent.com/pod-product-compliance
Lightning Source LLC
LaVergne TN
LVHW041333080426
835512LV00006B/431